CYBERWARS

Espionage on the Internet

CYBERWARS

Espionage on the Internet

JEAN GUISNEL

Foreword by
Winn Schwartau

Translated from the French by
Gui Masai

PLENUM TRADE · NEW YORK AND LONDON

Library of Congress Cataloging-in-Publication Data

Guisnel, Jean, 1951-
  [Guerres dans le cyberespace. English]
  Cyberwars : espionage on the Internet / Jean Guisnel ; foreword by
Winn Schwartau ; translated from the French by Gui Masai.
    p. cm.
  Includes bibliographical references and index.
  ISBN 0-306-45636-2
  1. Computer crimes. 2. Computer security. 3. Information
superhighway--Security measures. 4. Internet (Computer network)-
-Security measures. 5. World Wide Web (Information retrieval
system)--Security measures. 6. Secret service. 7. Intelligence
service. 8. Business intelligence. I. Title.
HV6773.G8513 1997
364.16'8--dc21   97-29521
                                                    CIP

For Geneviève, Carole, and Héloïse

ISBN 0-306-45636-2

The original version of this volume was published in French under the
title *Guerres dans le cyberespace: Services secrets et Internet,* © 1995
Editions La Découverte, Paris, France.

© 1997 Plenum Press, New York
Plenum Press is a Division of Plenum Publishing Corporation
233 Spring Street, New York, N.Y. 10013-1578
http://www.plenum.com

10 9 8 7 6 5 4 3 2 1

Printed in the United States of America

Taking Heat For Being Too Fast Forward

On March 4, 1990, I took a shower.

Not that this was a singular event; it wasn't even a Saturday. But this one shower stands out in my mind as a beginning. A new beginning for me. A new beginning for this country, and indeed, a new beginning for what was going to become an industry for tens of thousands of others world wide.

This shower began like all other showers. Wet and warm. Perfect, because I do my best thinking with torrents of water cascading over my head.

On this particular March morning my mind wandered and lazed into a semi-hypnogogic state, that indefinable place between asleep and awake. That place where a dream is so real one could swear a lifetime of vivid experiences had transpired in but a half a minute.

But this "dream"; this "vision" if you will, was different. It wasn't about mountains and lakes and pine trees in a *Sound of Music* setting. It was about war.

I saw a computer virus of anthropomorphic proportions intelligently targeting its next victim. I saw this virus call its friends, and with logistic support and reinforcements descend upon one unsuspecting victim after the other, each to fall helplessly as the viral army marched on.

The water continued to cascade as the battle played out before my mind's eye. The viruses were then joined by Sniffers, software designed to eavesdrop upon and invisibly abscond with the most closely guarded secrets. The digital cavalry galloped in with more malicious software meant to take control of an entire network, functioning in harmonic sympathy with the other combatant forces.

But it didn't stop there. As the movie in my mind played into the second scene I watched in abject fascination, wondering where this storehouse of knowledge was coming from and where it was headed. Silicon chips with a bad attitude joined the other virtual soldiers in their blitzkrieg to victory over my imagined victims.

Then the water chilled and I was shocked back into the comatose reality of a pre-coffee dawn. Yet I could recall what I had seen and replay it scene by scene.

And I called it Information Warfare.

In 1989, I published a paper in *Security Magazine* and in other security related magazines on how computer viruses can be embedded within word processing, spread sheets, and data bases, and did not need to infect software programs themselves. I suggested some solutions to what I predicted would develop into a formidable problem. It was met with skepticism.

And now today? Word macro viruses are the biggest malicious software industry by a factor of ten.

When Congress invited me to testify in June of 1991, the Pentagon didn't warn me that I was treading in classified areas. Nor did they tell me that they weren't exactly in favor of a private sector person figuring out their innermost secrets. I had been asked by the government to come to Congressman Dan Glickman's committee which was investigating the Computer Security Act and "shake congressmen to their very core." And with that in mind, I prepared my testimony, submitted it, and was looking forward to presenting my view on the current state of security.

"If we don't begin to take security seriously," I told the committee, "we face the prospect of an Electronic Pearl Harbor." I won't embarrass the other speakers who were there that day, but to a man, they said that "Mr. Schwartau is overstating the case," and they didn't believe in the sober prognostications I had put forth. To a man, they all today have made a terrific amount of money by cashing in on those prognostications by developing products, as, step by step, each one has come true.

Yesterday it was Information Security. Today, it's Information Warfare.

In April of 1994 the British unsuccessfully tried to ban my first book by the same title. That book caused quite a stir and as a result I was invited to speak at dozens of high-clearance U.S. military facilities and then suddenly uninvited "because someone at the Pentagon has it in for you." It took months, and in some cases years, to see behind Door #2; my military and intelligence supporters had to go through extraordinary measures to get me past the guards and inside buildings that don't officially exist. In one super-classified, highly initialed building, two armed guards were assigned to me, with the edict, "if he gets within twenty feet of a computer, shoot." Damn good thing the men's room used manual flushers!

And so it went. Then in April of 1997 MS-NBC (that's the Microsoft-NBC alliance) headlined an on-line show on the subject with "Information Warfare: A Myth?" and a captioned illustration that beatified it as "An Elaborate Hoax?" Most of the media still doesn't get it.

Finally, I was to receive the biggest compliment one can receive: President Clinton created the Infrastructure Protection Task Force to find a mechanism with which to combat civilian Information Warfare, a monument to the concept of a National Information Policy. The recognition that the United States does indeed face a host of new threats to which we must rapidly respond was at last becoming part of the political landscape.

As yesterday's future hits today's headlines I still think about tomorrow. One military outfit came to me and asked, "What about Information Warfare in the year 2010?" I responded, "If you wait that long, we lose."

Another group of military and intelligence experts flew me to an isolated swamp in the middle of the summer to ask what war was going to be like in the years 2020 and 2025. I told them, "You will have little recourse, little ability to fight. You will not be able to strike back at the aggressors because they will be more invisible than ever, and their weapons will not strike at bridges or airplanes or computers. War of the future will again be people versus people, person versus person, bypassing the traditional nation-state entirely. War of the future will be non-nuclear but everyone will have the weapons to destroy and even melt his neighbor." And then I proceeded to describe the technology that would accomplish this somewhat apocalyptic vision.

Too many people still believe that Information Warfare, or Cyber Espionage, or whatever we choose to call it, is a myth. That there has been progress is evidenced by this marvelous book by Jean Guisnel, who I am proud to call both friend and associate.

When I first read Jean's book, I sat back enthralled and I marveled at what he has achieved. He has taken a highly complex subject, a topic with so many different facets, and portrayed it such that the average person can understand it—clearly and succinctly. He has taken the well-defined taxonomy of Information Warfare and brought it to a level where everybody can see just how important these issues are to our national identity, and perhaps survival:

Class I: Personal Information Warfare. In Cyberspace you are guilty until proven innocent.

Class II: Economic and Industrial Espionage. The policies of the U.S. government are such that we actually encourage and invite it.

Class III: Terrorism. The Military. Electronic Civil Defense. Infrastructure Collapse.

Jean has made it all simple, accessible, and understandable. He takes the key aspects of the nature of Class II Information Warfare and tells us a story that even my octogenarian Aunt Libby would both enjoy and understand.

My hat is off to Jean Guisnel. *Cyberwars* is the most readable and clearly condensed history of

Information Warfare, Cyberterrorism, and Computer Espionage I have ever seen. *Cyberwars* is an absolute must read for everyone with a stake in the future.

Read it.

Enjoy it.

Heed it.

Winn Schwartau
Seminole, Florida

Contents

Some Background
on the Internet

The year 1969 was nothing if not eventful: Neil Armstrong took man's first step onto the moon, the Woodstock festival brought free love and rock and roll to a sleepy New York town, and the New York Mets became the youngest franchise ever to win the World Series. However, 1969 may be remembered for an event more important than any of these, an event that, at the time, went wholly unobserved. In 1969 the Internet was born.

The idea behind it was simple: to link computers in a few scientific laboratories across the United States. However, it quickly became clear that for such an idea to succeed, some very high-powered help would be required. That assistance came from the Pentagon, in the form of its Advanced Research Project Agency (ARPA), whose first network would soon be christened ARPANET.[1] Nonetheless, at the time, the idea of computer networking would have seemed off the wall, for good reason: computers in 1969 were big slow machines that operated in isolation, spoke various languages, were made of huge components, and had limited number-crunching power. At that time the only thing they did particularly well was break down. Every button pushed set in motion a squad of technicians who, when they weren't repairing them, were tearing their hair out over them. A building full of computers was required to process the information that sent Apollo 11's three-man crew to the moon.

Robert Taylor and Joseph C. R. Licklider, two computer scientists from UCLA, during the mid-1960s, came up with the idea that computers would one day cease to be closed circuits and would communicate with one another. Shortly thereafter they put their theory into practice. On November 21, 1969, computers at UC Santa Barbara, the Stanford Research Institute, and the University of Utah were all linked at UCLA, and a message was sent from one computer to another within the network.

The Pentagon, which did not hesitate to finance the program from 1966 forward, still had to figure out how to put into practice something that was barely an idea—the linking of remote computers so that they could communicate with each other. In their book on the birth of the Internet, Katie Hafner and Matthew Lyon report a rumor that circulated during the era: the network was being designed to withstand a nuclear Armageddon. Were such a desperate situation to arise, the network would need to continue to function, however many Soviet warheads might detonate on American soil.[2] They needed to devise "nodes" through which the messages, now divided into "packets"—fragments or bits of the original message—would pass, each of which would follow a different route to the same destination. A nuclear explosion that might destroy various nodes would not wipe out the entire web; therefore the packets could always take another route to their destination, provided they still had a pathway and that the destination itself had survived. Today's Internet still functions this way—when sending electronic messages or e-mail, you can never be certain what path the packets will take to their common destination.

The scientific community was the first (and for a long time the only) user of these networks, which quickly became forums for debate and discussion ranging from the scientific to the political and cultural. Usenet was created, a network of intellectuals using technology to promote varied and lively debate within different forums that we now call *newsgroups*. Each network, however, remained autonomously managed, each with its own name, procedures, structures, and members.

The idea of intercomputer communication may seem quite simple to us, but it took nearly a quarter of a century to work out the massive difficulties in what has now become a network that, according to a study conducted in 1995, consists of over 30 million computers in North America alone. The Internet Society (ISOC) offers somewhat different numbers, claiming that in July of 1996 just 13 million computers were connected across the globe. ISOC further stated that the number of new users is increasing by 30% per year: by the turn of the millennium, there should be over 100 million linked users throughout the world. Regardless of the exact current figure, more people than ever before are signing on.

Initially, the technological limitations of 1969 dictated the transmission of brief texts only. To make matters worse, these transmitted texts would still be in the language of the sender's computer— not the receiver's. Thus, neither computer could make sense of the contents of the other network: it was all gibberish. Clearly, the biggest hurdle became the defining of a common language that would bridge the gap between autonomous networks. Thus *protocols* were born—standardized procedures for regulating data transmission between computers— no matter how different their sizes, strengths, or operating systems. These protocols made universal communication possible and allowed the transmission of text and data.

Protocols are the basic building blocks of the Internet. In the beginning there were two: TCP (Transmission Control Protocol) and IP (Internet Protocol). Now there are over a hundred. Led by Vint Cerf, a former UCLA student during the glory days of ARPANET, the Internet Society has helped network organizers to set up their own basic parameters and protocols, such as standardizing an e-mail system.[3] Born out of thin air in 1969, the network that spawned the Internet took its time in bearing offspring of its own. In the beginning, there simply weren't very many computers. Those that existed were clumsy behemoths in big corporations and laboratories, whose strange green symbols flashing across black screens were largely incomprehensible to anyone without a Ph.D. in computer science. The memorization of the commands alone would have been enough to give most of us a migraine.

The first bit of good news along the road to simplification came in the early 1980s with the advent of personal computers mere mortals could operate, like Apple's Macintosh line. Bill Gates, founder of Microsoft, pioneered basic operating systems like MS-DOS and later the Windows graphic interface, both destined for IBM computers and compatibles. These developments marked the explosion of the microcomputer and the first golden age of the Internet, made possible by the drop in personal computer prices and the dramatic increase in the power of the machines.

By the end of the 1980s, connecting to the Internet was still tricky business, the protocols were difficult to understand and operate, and the screens that linked one area to another were hopelessly antiquated. The Internet was not yet user-friendly.

In 1989 a new wave crested in the Internet ocean: the invention of the World Wide Web (WWW). It was created by Timothy Berners-Lee at CERN (European Center for Nuclear Research),[4] a European nuclear research facility in Geneva, Switzerland.[5] The idea behind it was to provide netsurfers with an easier means of access than protocols had previously made possible. A "Web site" would be made up of a group of servers within the larger frame of the World Wide Web, and all those within *it* would be able to move quickly and freely between its constituent parts. The concept that would allow for such rapid, convenient transit was called *hypertext*.[6] Users looking, say, at an on-screen table of contents, could click on a particular chapter and be sent there directly without having to execute a complex series of protocols, the protocols being invisibly imbedded within the World Wide Web. Accessing the Internet had become as easy as snapping your fingers, and the results were truly amazing: servers could even offer hypertext links to other servers. With a push of a button, a user in Paris could be connected in a few seconds to a Japanese server, and beyond, making any number of stops around the globe.

Then in 1993 with the arrival of Mosaic, the Internet became a part of the daily lives of millions of users. Mosaic, and soon after Netscape Navigator, an even more user-friendly program, are software programs created by Marc Andreessen that, for the first time, give even beginning netsurfers the ability to take full advantage of the Internet. In keeping with the philosophy of those who have created and developed the Internet, thousands of copies per day were initially downloaded free of charge by users all over the world. This allowed everyone—businesses, universities, databases, as well as individual users everywhere—to have access to all the varied offerings found on the web. All that was needed was a computer, a modem, a phone line, and a local phone number set up by a provider to dial into the Internet. From there, with a computer running Mosaic or Netscape Navigator, users were free to surf the net, connecting to a world of providers for the cost of a local phone call and a nominal monthly fee paid to the provider for offering access.

The bigger networks had finally spawned smaller ones that allowed users of all sizes to travel along hypertextual roadways, carrying virtual cargo with them as varied as that on any actual superhighway, ranging from the essential to the frivolous, from the ponderous to the whimsical, all in electronic form. Instantaneous electronic transfer was replacing red-eye flights and cross-continental treks, with data circling the globe at the speed of light. The amount of information being shipped defies understanding, and out of such quantity a new philosophy of communication was born: from the comfort of one's own home, with a microcomputer, anyone can go anywhere. And since most computers that users hook up to are hardly Fort Knox, almost anything is fairly accessible, not only to individuals, of course, but to their countries as well. And their secret services too, most of which have already begun to inhabit the shadowy world of the Information War.

Currently, two different lines of communication link computers to one another. For the average citizen, which is to say most of us, there are the world's phone companies, with more than 600 million subscribers across the planet. Through millions of miles of copper wiring, the electrons pass relatively quickly and easily. However, computer professionals as well as scientists, businesses, and the military all have better connections. These access routes allow for very high speed information transfer. Your Internet provider is connected to these specialized connections, and stuffs its subscribers through a ground-floor window it rents in what is a much more massive structure. Since 1995, ISDN (Integrated Services Digital Network) technology has been of increasing interest to some users. Via higher quality copper telephone wires, data can travel at 64 Kbps,[7] a rate sufficient to allow for the transfer of voice and video, as well as the downloading of text and data at more sensible speeds. Images transferred via ISDN are far more crude than those of broadcast quality— the level of detail we are accustomed to seeing on television. Even with the use of image compression software, a speed of 2 million bps (Megabits or Mbps) would be necessary to achieve such quality. Faster networks are out there, but they are far from being as common as the copper wires in homes everywhere. A new U.S. network called VBNS (Very High Speed Backbone Network Service) offers connections at up to 155 Mbps by using a technology called ATM (Asynchronous Transfer Mode) along with fiber-optic cables. Although ATM only recently seemed like the technology of the future, it soon could be dethroned by a yet faster technology: Ethernet, which acheives speeds of 1 billion bits per second (Gbps), a full Gigabit.

And then there's the future. The Internet, a tool which allows for computers and their users to communicate, respond to, and acquire information at great distances, is able to transmit sound and images. But the current speeds across copper telephone cables aren't fast enough to adequately transmit real-time films and television programs. Various cable companies have been scrambling to prepare themselves for the future, believing that their fate rests in the development of high-speed Internet access via their existing cable lines. This means cable access could make the catch-phrase of the 1990s—the Information Superhighway (or as the Germans put it, the Infobahn)—a reality. The benefit of this type of connection is that in most homes it already exists: the cable companies are waiting for the advent of multimedia computers, a new product just beginning to trickle onto the market.These computers, the first of which appeared in the spring of 1996, have been dubbed NCs (Network Computers). The idea behind the name resides in their innovative conception of software. No longer would these computers have hard drives or CD-ROMs filled with programs. Instead, the computers would access the programs from the network to which they would be connected. With such a basic configuration, the cost of such computers could be reduced to around $500.[8] Hybrids of familiar household items—the telephone, television, and personal computer—these machines will be able to receive digital video images instantly, through the Internet. The biggest difference between this system of tomorrow (which is already here) and what most of us use now is the flexibility that high-speed transfer offers. Users will be able to interact with other users in real time, to play games or order films and other products that they can use right there, immediately, in the comfort of their multimedia hookup. Television will have become wholly interactive.

I've made every attempt here to keep technical jargon to a minimum, but a minimum that will give users new to the Internet the information necessary to explore it on their own. Therefore, when discussing various sites, organizations or services currently available, I have usually included a footnote giving the address of a corresponding Web site. I've tested all of them and they should work well for you. As for the specific steps of how to hook up to the Internet, as I've said, you need a computer, a modem, a phone line, and a provider. The number of providers is proliferating, and though most of them use Netscape for software or Microsoft's Internet Explorer, which is gaining a larger market share day by day, some online services like America Online and

Prodigy offer Web access too, although of a generally less satisfying nature (slower and less convenient). The best advice I can offer on which provider to choose is to shop around for a package of perks you like. It's a competitive market, and you should have no difficulty finding a suitable provider.

The various addresses I provide throughout the book (the CIA, the president of the United States, etc.) should provide some additional avenues of investigation for interested readers. If you have any comments, you may send them directly to me at my e-mail address: jguisnel@calva.net.

1
The New Secret Services

On February 21, 1994, at the corner of Quebec Street and Nelly Curtis Drive, in Arlington, Virginia, a man with a mustache eased his Jaguar to a stop. He didn't have a choice: another car was blocking his way, strangely motionless at a green light. Sitting there, he could've been an accountant, or maybe an insurance salesman, some guy in a big car, wide-eyed behind heavy glasses. And after he'd been yanked from inside and found his hands suddenly slammed against the hood by powerful arms that had come out of nowhere, this diminutive CIA chief who loved a drink perhaps a little more than he should have didn't look like a big shot at all. When the counterespionage agents were cuffing him and giving him the lowdown on why he was being arrested, he said the only thing he could think of: "There must be some mistake. Espionage, me?"

Aldrich Ames, the greatest traitor the CIA had bred since its creation at the end of the Second World War, had over the course of a decade caused the arrest of dozens of the CIA's Russian operatives, ten of whom had later been executed. Just five years after the fall of the Berlin Wall, Ames's life sentence symbolically marked the end of the Cold War for the American and Russian intelligence services. Past debts had been settled. The war between the "defenders of the free world" and "the communist aggressors" would never recur in the same form, even though history has a mysterious tendency of repeating itself.

On the Ruins of the Cold War

At the beginning of the summer of 1993, six months before Ames's arrest, CIA director James Woolsey and Evgueni Primakov, the director of Russia's Federal Security Service,[1] sat down together to share a good bottle of wine and to discuss their new collaboration. There was plenty to talk about, from how to fight a mafia that had already been accused of selling nuclear materials across Russian borders to how best to suppress drug trafficking and money laundering. But this was just the starting point: there was also Russia's recent disclosure—partial, of course—of files concerning their support of various terrorist organizations since the late 1960s.

Claude Silberzahn, director of France's espionage wing, the DGSE,[2] was the first Western intelligence service chief to have received Primakov. They met on a sunny day in Paris in 1992 at CAT headquarters,[3] in the old barracks on boulevard Mortier, better known to the world by its nickname, *la Piscine*, the Pool. After having welcomed Primakov and a half-dozen high-ups from the former KGB, Silberzahn wrote of the feelings that had struck the French top brass, and which couldn't have been very far from those felt by their American colleagues a few months later: "Our top people felt no antagonism towards them. Incredible curiosity, yes, but no ill will. I can hardly believe I'm writing this but during those days, I felt a strange sense of happiness around the place, like that feeling you sometimes get around the dinner table when relatives visit whom you haven't seen for a long time, because of some long-standing falling out. There was also a certain nostalgia that prevailed, the feeling that it was the end of an era. An age old conflict was coming to a close. It was as though all the cold sweats and spilled blood had been forgotten . . . ."[4]

Seventy years of Soviet Communism provided The West with a highly convenient rationale for, among other things, the birth and development of intelligence-gathering organizations of considerable scope. Forged in the pre-war years during the rise of Nazism and steeled during the struggle with it, modern espionage focused its undivided attention on the Communist world. During this period the great modern secret services were created, most of which survive today in their original form. The CIA was established in 1945 and was built on the foundations of the war's information-gathering apparatus, the OSS (Office of Strategic Services). The CIA's mandate was to gather information about individuals (HUMINT, for human intelligence) and to execute secret initiatives. It was supplemented in 1952 by order of President Harry Truman with the NSA (National Security Agency), located in Fort Mead, Maryland, a branch devoted solely to the gathering of technical information (TECHINT, for technical intelligence). Today, the NSA employs 40,000 people and has an annual operating budget of $3.5 billion. And that, officially, is all that we know about the agency: it is submerged in a depth of secrecy that boggles the mind.[5]

When new employees join the NSA, the first information that they are given involves the perpetuation of this secrecy. Chris Goggans (aka Erik Bloodaxe), the former editor of *Phrack*, an underground magazine catering to hackers, took immense pleasure in publishing a large part of the NSA's security manual, in which the chief of security, Philip T. Pease, outlines the agency's principles for its latest initiates: "While it is impossible to estimate in actual dollars and cents the value of the work being conducted by this Agency, the information to which you will have access at NSA is without question critically important to the defense of the United States. Since this information may be useful only if it is kept secret, it requires a very special measure of protection. The specific nature of this protection is set forth in various agency security regulations and directives. The total NSA Security Program, however, extends beyond these regulations. It is based upon the concept that security begins as a state of mind. The program is designed to develop an appreciation of the need to protect information vital to the national defense, and to foster the development of a level of awareness which will make security more than routine compliance with regulations. At times, security practices and procedures cause personal inconvenience. They take time and effort and on occasion may make it necessary for you to voluntarily forgo some of your usual personal prerogatives. But your compensation for the inconvenience is the knowledge that the work you are accomplishing at NSA, within a framework of sound security practices, contributes significantly to the defense and continued security of the United States of America."[6]

In the name of defending the security of the United States of America, the NSA intercepts virtually everything that electricity or radio waves can carry. Communications from all civil satellites are intercepted, underwater cables are tapped, electromagnetic waves are captured, wherever they are around the world. The NSA has its own boats and planes, as well as satellites dedicated to electronic espionage, all part of its ELINT or electronic intelligence program, itself a part of TECHINT. The NSA also works in collaboration with Britain's GCHQ (Government Communications Headquarters, to which it is linked by the secret UKUSA alliance) and ASIO (Australian Security Intelligence Organization), to whom the NSA subcontracts more minor missions in Europe, the Middle East, and Asia. And the NSA also uses some of the most powerful computers in the world, computers designed for their needs. The NSA was computer designer Seymour Cray's first client, and it remains the biggest buyer of Cray computers. In short, the NSA has more than enough hands to keep busy with dominating the global electronomy.

Naturally, the Internet has become one of the NSA's favorite victims: it has practically hijacked the whole thing. If no serious business should trust its correspondence to the network, and if no government should send along sensitive information, the reason lies in the NSA's increasingly close watch over communications crossing American soil, most of which unwittingly pass through their information filters at their headquarters in Fort Meade, Maryland. A shy electron set in motion in some distant corner of the planet cannot seriously hope to escape notice.

During the era of the Soviet Union and the Cold War, the NSA proved to be the most intrepid observer of the Communist world: it didn't matter that an iron curtain had been drawn around its borders and that actual penetration of its frontiers by agents had become practically impossible. The Soviet government agencies, including the military and state-run production facilities, still had to communicate *intra muros*. By telephone, radio, or telegraph, by radio waves passing over ground or in the air, by plane or satellite radar searching the skies, virtually all that was sent out was intercepted, or could have been, by the NSA—and still can be. To achieve such an end, the U.S. Navy used nuclear submarines to execute one of the most stupefying surveillance coups of the Cold War: the installation of an eavesdropping device, code-named "Ivy Bell," on a Soviet underwater telephone cable off their Pacific coast.

The New Breed of Espionage

Although the intelligence-gathering services of many countries are involved in a new breed of espionage, the NSA is at the heart of things, operating on a scale that dwarfs its closest rival. The former Soviet Union was the NSA's only real competitor, using nearly 350,000 operatives in intelligence gathering and analysis. But that, as they say, was then.

Because of the extraordinary revolution underway in the communications technologies of the late twentieth century, there is scarcely any source of information—whether intellectual, political, industrial, military, or commercial—that is not within reach. Even if the printed page does endure as a means of conveying information, more and more frequently texts are being sent across the globe electronically at incredible speeds: a novel can been sent via modem to another computer in a matter of seconds. All the while, information is accumulating invisibly on hard drives, an ordinary office computer stores the equivalent of tens of thousands of pages. Data bases across the planet have become vast repositories of human knowledge, and the number of individuals turning to them for information is growing phenomenally. Some of these new information nexuses are public and therefore accessible to everyone, either free of charge or at a nominal fee. Others are private and their contents confidential, no matter how much some people would be willing to pay for access to them. Needless to say, it is precisely these data bases that are the envy of the world's secret services, who more and more are enlisting the aid of information hackers to storm them.

It is a considerable understatement to say that the world's secret services haven't remained indifferent to the information revolution; quite the contrary, the revolution has become their daily bread. With 30 million computers interconnected throughout the world, those adept enough to insinuate their way deep into the core of this virtual world have access to a boggling array of private information. And gaining access is what the NSA has spent the past quarter-century learning to do.

Of course, the old school of espionage still has some sunny days of secret-agenting to look forward to—missions impossible, showdowns hidden deep in misty foreign forests—the fun stuff that shows up in Hollywood blockbusters. The most basic element to be found in any such story of international hijinks is the wiretap. Taps have been a regular part of the police arsenals since shortly after Mr. Graham Bell pioneered the electrical transmission of speech in 1876, and the principle behind them remains much the same today for the pirates who intercept messages along the ever-widening information highway. What makes this old-fashioned idea relevant to us is how it is being applied to the surveillance and expert perusal of digital information traveling within the borders of the world's countries; above all, what is of particular interest to the secret services are information transfers that flaunt the traditional notions of borders, billions of bits traveling day and night across communications networks like electrical impulses moving through the nervous system of one vast body. Electrons don't show passports at customs. In cyberspace—the world of digital network communication as coined by novelist William Gibson in his *Neuromancer*—all boundaries are virtual.[7]

Professor William T. Warner, a former naval intelligence officer and professor of political science at the University of Kentucky, is also an adjunct fellow at the Center for Strategic and International Studies in Washington. As such, he is one of the world's most knowledgeable scholars on the evolution of modern espionage. Recently, in a discussion of the new factors which render the United States more vulnerable to new forms of espionage, Professor Warner discussed emerging technologies: "The technical factor involves those aspects of the electronic 'information revolution' which have digitalized information generation, storage, transfer, and reception while drastically reducing the size, cost, and operational complexity of equipment used to control and manage data. When secrets were recorded on documents locked away in safes, stealing information relied upon classic espionage techniques, such as physical theft of actual plans or documents, bribing or compromising individuals in possession of the desired knowledge, or other techniques which risk "leaving tracks" and ultimate detection. Stealing information in the 'digital age,' however, can be accomplished merely by intercepting formatted data at some point, either where it is stored, or as it is transmitted. The same technology which has made possible the development of digital information management has also bred relatively surreptitious systems of electronic snooping: unauthorized penetration of protected databases, illegal interception of digitalized transmission signals (which NSA does legally), and other methods."[8]

This evolution has prompted upheaval within the secret services: the formidable technical apparatuses developed out of the depths of the Cold War and put to use with a policeman's pragmatism have clashed with a reality that is difficult to accept by those adherents of an order founded on the idea of general surveillance of the citizenry. The relative transparency of the Internet allows almost anyone to read anyone else's mail. And without too much more difficulty, one can also infiltrate the personal systems of others, perusing contents that should certainly remain off-limits. In so doing, we have finally obliterated one of the last strongholds of privacy in our constantly shrinking world.

But every poison has its antidote. Parallel to the joyous, rapid, anarchic birth of global communications networks has been the development of new tools to protect our personal liberties. Imaginative computer scientists and mathematicians have developed a variety of cryptological means of protecting privileged network communications. These virtual locks have been distributed free of charge and at the speed of light to millions of users around the globe. And the world's various secret services, with the NSA leading the way, have been trying to fight this growing trend. Such are the high-stakes growing pains of cyberspace's adolescence.

The Fight Against Terrorism

Since the end of the Cold War, the secret services have been finding better uses for their time and energy than the bugging of former rivals. In France a host of new issues is being addressed. Since the early 1980s, the secret services have focused their attentions on fighting terrorism originating in the Middle East. Syria, Iran, and Libya have all been implicated in various international incidents, particularly on French soil, including a wave of attacks throughout 1986 and the bombing of a UTA DC-10 on September 19, 1989. On July 25, 1995, during the height of the summer tourist season, a bomb exploded in the Parisian commuter rail line (the same train line travelers take to the airport and to Euro-Disney). Just one month later on August 17, another bomb went off on Paris's main tourist drag, the Champs-Elysées.

After these first two attacks, France was hit by a series of terrorist bombings that did not stop until November of 1995, after eight people had been killed and 130 injured. Khalid Kelkal, one of the leaders of a terrorist group that had divisions in three French cities, was killed by the police on September 29, 1995. In order to trace their way to the man at the top, to find all of the members of the Algerian terrorist group (GIA, Groupe Islamique Armé) that had entered France illegally, and to reconstruct the elaborate web of alliances the terrorists used to execute their orders, the French police made use of all they had learned in forty years of tracking Soviet agents during the Cold War: hideouts, tails, and the mobilization of dozens of counterespionage specialists adept at listening in and interception. Such need-based endeavors allowed for the DGSE and the DST, the two major French specialized services, to evolve away from Cold War activities toward the exigencies of modern terrorist activity. In addition to the elaborate technological systems at their disposal, these bureaus didn't hesitate to send agents into the field alone. It was in this solitary capacity that General Philippe Rondot, a French counterespionage ace, hunted and captured the noted terrorist Carlos the Jackal in Sudan in August of 1994 . For fifteen years the Venezuelan mercenary had eluded the world's various secret services while working for some of the Middle East's most violent terrorist groups. It seems that the U.S. secret services first spotted him in Sudan, perhaps as a part of an NSA initiative. Then Rondot succeeded in actually tracking him down and photographing him before hauling him off to France, where he still sits in a Parisian prison awaiting trial. Unfortunately, this tragic series of attacks on the French capital continued on December 3, 1996, with the explosion of a bomb in the RER commuter train in Port Royal station. Four people were killed, and 126 were wounded.

But not all French agents are lone wolves prowling the Middle Eastern wilderness, roving back alleys with a baguette, cigarette, and beret and thumbing their noses at the Russian agents, the CIA, and Mossad. In fact, for more than a decade, Western observers had been able to intercept and decrypt messages between Iranian embassies and Tehran. A few days after the assassination of former Iranian prime minister Chapour Bakhtiar on June 6, 1991, near Paris, the antiterrorist judge Jean-Louis Bruguière learned that the suspected killers had called their base from the Iranian embassy in Paris to report their success. When the story was leaked to the French press and the general public became aware of the conversation between the killers and their colleagues in Tehran, the Iranians knew once and for all that their communications were being intercepted and decoded, or as experts say, *decrypted.*

This major information-gathering coup wasn't won by the sweat and toil of cryptographers: it came far more easily than that. The Swiss company Crypto AG, which had designed and sold the cryptography systems Iran was using for its top-secret communications, had also delivered copies of the Iranian keys to the Swiss secret service. They, in turn, had generously distributed copies to their colleagues working for other secret services throughout the world. Or so says Hans Bülher, an executive of Crypto AG who was jailed in Iran for most of 1992 after news of this affair broke.

The United States, whose domestic experience with terrorism was nonexistent during the 1980s, has quickly begun to develop expertise. The first hit on an American concern occurred on December 21, when a Pan Am 747 was bombed over Lockerbie, Scotland, and all onboard were killed. Since then, terrorists have hit the World Trade Center (February 26, 1993), the federal courthouse in Oklahoma City (in 1995), and the Olympic Games in Atlanta. Though the perpetrators of these horrors have been both home-grown and foreign, it is clear that in the age of the Unabomber, American soil is no longer safe from the villainy of random violence.

As a result, the American secret services have been busy trying to staunch the flow by all means possible. This has required a rapid adaptation to the realities of stopping terrorism on domestic soil. The NSA isn't the only government agency left to deal with such high-profile demands. The NRO (National Reconnaissance Office) has existed since 1960, although its existence was secret until 1992. Charged with keeping track of U.S. spy satellites and their harvests, the NRO spends $5 billion annually trying to intercept the bad news before it costs lives. The

NRO recently experienced some rough waters familiar to secret services: it had begun to think it could function without executive approval. In February of 1996, CIA director John M. Deutch and secretary of defense William J. Perry took drastic action when they discovered the unusually high costs associated with the construction of the NRO's new headquarters, as well as some excessive budget demands. This led to the dismissal of director Jeffrey K. Harris and his assistant Jimmy D. Hill. The affair came on the heels of vocal disapproval of the agency that had been leveled a few days earlier by Arlen Specter, chairman of the Senate Select Intelligence Committee.

The American Way

Despite America's significant losses at the hands of terrorists, the various branches of the United States intelligence services spend a much larger portion of their annual budget ($30 billion in 1997) on gathering economic information than they do on combating terrorism. At first, they attempted to fight against the spies who were infiltrating companies, as well as the countries that, on American soil, had undertaken initiatives to systematically pillage U.S. riches, all for the benefit of various private foreign firms. The Japanese have shown particular ability in this domain, unabashedly infiltrating various businesses and scouring them for information. No means has been beyond them: theft, purchase, bribery, occasionally even taking assistance from their government—passing papers along through the diplomatic pouch. The NSA's analysts were in a state of shock when they decoded and translated intercepted messages destined for Tokyo from the Mitsubishi Corporation's Washington office: they contained no less than the CIA's daily breakdown, a brief reserved for the president of the United States and members of the National Security Council. A few years earlier the Hitachi corporation penetrated IBM deeply, transmitting its plunder (encrypted in Japanese diplomatic code) via the Japanese consul in San Francisco. Nor have the Germans and the Israelis been outdone in this domain. The United States has accused the Germans of several break-ins into the SWIFT network (Society for World International Financial Transactions), which specializes in computer banking interconnection. In Israel, Mossad suppressed bids by various American aeronautic firms, allowing the national Israeli Aircraft Industries to sidestep their competitors to secure a spy-plane order worth $20 million.[9]

But the prize for best economic espionage on American soil goes to the French. The DGSE's spies have excelled in this capacity, so much so that they provoked a diplomatic incident between Paris and Washington during the 1970s. Alexandre de Marenches, nicknamed Porthos after the fat musketeer, was in the twilight years of his reign at the DGSE. At his behest, the heads of the agency had begun to plant young, very high level engineers (who were also DGSE agents) in various French subsidiaries of well-known American firms. The targets they chose betray the priorities of the era: two major electronics firms, IBM and Texas Instruments, as well as Corning Glass, one the world's leaders in the glass industry. At the time, Corning was researching and developing a promising technology—fiber optics—that has gone on to play a major role in the development of the information super highway. Over the years, other firms were targeted, mostly those in the aeronautics industry where competition was cutthroat: both Boeing and Bell Helicopter Textron were earmarked as they prepared to build a very interesting hybrid plane-helicopter, the V-22. The French also penetrated one of the industry's most innovative companies, Northrop, known for having managed to render its bombers invisible to radar with the pioneering F-117 and B-2. In short, advances were made upon all the experts in stealth technology, sometimes so successfully that moles were placed in their research teams.

Little by little, the French engineers became integral parts of the companies they had entered, some rising to positions of power and authority within the corporate hierarchies. The objective was clear: though never stated as such by anyone, they were there to steal commercial and industrial secrets that would allow competing French companies rapid technological advancement without massive research and development costs. The principal beneficiary of the DGSE's generosity was the electronics firm Bull, which, of course, denies any such complicity.

In 1988, with the French presidential campaign in full swing, America woke up. It was not immediately clear whether the French moles had been denounced from within or whether they had been rooted out. Either way, FBI agents got to many of them and told them that the agency knew exactly what they were up to. This led to something of a panic back in Paris, as well as furor among the politicians supposedly in charge. General François Mermet, then head of the DGSE, was asked to step down on March 23, 1989. His successor Claude Silberzahn's first job was to go to the United States to negotiate secretly with his American counterpart Robert Gates to arrange an honorable exit.

Since then the United States has taken an aggressive stance. Bill Clinton made a crackdown on these sorts of activities a rallying cry of his first presidential campaign. Once elected, however, he too put his intelligence people to work: if not officially, American espionage would now become a priority in an effort to advance American companies. His administration reckoned, with a touching unanimity and more than a little arrogance, that they had no other choice. Besides, they were only repaying their strategic and political friends, who were also their economic competitors, in kind. "US economic globalism has not only internationalized American business methods and processes, it has showcased American technology. Everybody wants it and tries to get it one way or the other. Most nations—friend or foe—have either used American technology as a springboard to development (France, Japan, e.g.), or become "hooked" on it for their very survival (the former USSR)."[10]

The Fight Against Money Laundering

Surveillance and analysis of communications networks have been the primary means of combating money laundering. Most intelligence services in the industrialized world have decided to invest heavily in hunting down the illicit financial flow, devoting political, law enforcement, and economic resources to that end. The American FinCen (Financial Crimes Enforcement Network) shares an enormous database with Great Britain's NCIN (National Criminal Intelligence Network), linking those fighting the trafficking of drugs to customs officials and banking regulation institutions, all similarly interested in alerting authorities of the movement of large sums of suspicious money. This mass of data goes through constant financial analysis and, above all, surveillance of the world interbank network SWIFT (Society for World International Financial Transactions)—an agency more or less tolerated by the various institutions, depending on their host countries.

But technology isn't everything. You still have to know what you're looking for. Estimates indicate that there is a disconcerting amount of drug money in motion. One of the few organizations to offer reliable statistics on the subject is the OECD's FATF (Financial Action Taskforce).[11] In 1990 the group estimated that drug sales were generating as much as $122 billion per year, 50%–75% of which could be slipped directly back into the economy unnoticed. But even with their access to such information, which includes actual interbank communications to pinpoint shady transactions, today's Western intelligence services sometimes find themselves in very delicate and complex situations.

Today, drug traffickers aren't outcasts hidden behind an iron curtain. They use cellular phones for their communications, the Internet for encoding secret messages, travel freely, and have multiple bank accounts in the finest financial institutions in the world. With the law of the market being what it is, they take great pleasure in making use of these prestigious palaces of corporate flattery, conducting business in them like any other client. This is where the secret services have met with great difficulties, as they have not yet found a way to deal with these insidious adversaries who play dirty on the same field as honest citizens. As the GAFI report would have it, "The implicated parties in these stupefyingly illegal activities inevitably manage to hold liquid assets or accounts receivable in these financial institutions, from whom, undoubtedly, they wish to hide their ties to illicit activities. In point of fact, we do not have enough information available to us in order to properly evaluate the bank liabilities tied to the laundering of money."[12] "Every year things get worse. In May of 1996 the FATF estimated that 300 billion dollars of illegal funds of all kinds circulate each year through banking networks. In 1997 the FATF's latest concern has to do with the use of digital cash allowing for anonymous and secure transactions, for law-abiding citizens and crooks alike."[13]

2
The First Cyberwarriors

With his long hair and neat beard, John Perry Barlow seems like an easygoing, down-to-earth guy. He's made a good living from the songs he wrote for the Grateful Dead (among others), and now owns a cattle ranch in Sublette County, Wyoming. At the end of 1989, he hooked up to the Internet on the advice of a musician friend and had his first experiences with other enthusiasts frequenting the WELL (Whole Earth 'Lectronic Link). He also had his first encounters with the police.

The Electronic Frontier Foundation Enters the Fray

On January 15, 1990, AT&T's telephone network was experiencing serious operating difficulties across the northeastern United States. Barlow, among others, thought it might have had something to do with hackers breaking into AT&T's computers. But unbeknownst to him, he had become a suspect in the unfolding investigation. The Feds suspected that he belonged to the NuPrometheus network that had acquired and distributed—illegally, of course—many source codes for the ROM used in Apple's Macintosh computers.

In April of 1990, after three hours of rather dry conversation with FBI agent Richard Baxter, a specialist in livestock theft who had come out from Rock Springs, Barlow was convinced that the Feds were in a panic and that one of his fundamental rights—to communicate freely with whomever he wished—had become suspect in the eyes of those upholding the law: "I realized in the course of this interview that I was seeing, in microcosm, the entire law enforcement structure of the United States. Agent Baxter was hardly alone in his puzzlement about the legal, technical, and metaphorical nature of datacrime. I also found in his strugles a framework for understanding a series of recent Secret Service raids on some young hackers I'd met in a *Harper's* magazine forum on computers and freedom. And it occurred to me that this might be the beginning of a great paroxysm of govermental confusion during which everyone's liberties would become at risk."[1]

The Net was an ideal forum for airing his concerns. He brought them directly onto the network, ranting and raving to his heart's content. In the burgeoning cyberspace, the echoes of his protest hit home with another rich man. A millionaire author of several software programs before he was thirty, Mitchell Kapor had founded Lotus in 1981, which he turned around and sold in 1983 for a tidy sum. (Its new owners managed over the next ten years to capture 34% of the network communications software market, its closest competitor Microsoft only managing a 12% share. In 1995, based on this dominance, IBM bought the company from its owners for an astounding $3.3 billion.) By 1989, Kapor was semiretired and spending much of his time on the Net. He, too, had been visited by the FBI, at his home in Massachusetts, so Barlow's messages found an ally in him. They met and, "They spoke about consciousness and the Net and the threat to civil liberties. Both believed they were on the threshold of a netborne Great Work, a wiring together of humanity that would restructure civilization. They talked for three hours, then fostered their face-to-face connection with e-mail, agreeing that they should do something together. But what?"[2]

An idea quickly took shape: they would establish a forum. That forum has become the conscience of the Internet, the necessary interlocutor for American authorities, for everything having to do with liberty on the network.

Through their vocal stands on free speech, Kapor and Barlow are well known to Vice President Al Gore, the great exponent of the information superhighway. Even in 1990 when they announced the formation of their organization, there was an air of prophesy to the direction they charted: "In its present condition, Cyberspace is a frontier region, populated by the few hardy technologists who can tolerate the austerity of its savage computer interfaces, incompatible communications protocols, proprietary barricades, cultural and legal ambiguities, and general lack of useful maps or metaphors. Certainly, the old concepts of property, expression, identity, movement, and context, based as they are on physical manifestation, do not apply succinctly in a world where there can be none. Sovereignty over this new world is also not well defined. Large institutions already lay claim to large fiefdoms, but most of the actual natives are solitary and independent, sometimes to the point of sociopathy. It is, therefore, a perfect breeding ground for both outlaws and vigilantes."[3]

The birth of the Electronic Frontier Foundation (EFF) had the immediate consequence of causing cases implicating federal security services to burst out of the woodwork, most of which had previously been ignored by the press. "The media hadn't covered the story because they didn't know about it. Or, at least, they didn't understand the issues."[4]

The fabulously wealthy founders of the EFF put their wherewithal in service of the cause, using top lawyers to defend hackers who were being pursued by federal officials, such as Steve Jackson, a producer of information-based games, who had had all of his materials seized by the Secret Service in order to block the introduction of his game *Cyberpunk*, which the government claimed would promote information hacking. A gigantic police operation, code-named Sun Devil, that had been launched on May 8, 1990, provoked one of the first public reactions by the EFF: in fourteen U.S. cities, forty computers and *twenty-three thousand* diskettes were seized from teenagers. Craig Neidorf also got help from the EFF: this clever young man was alleged to have published a portion of a telephone company's internal documents in an online magazine popular with hackers called *Phrack*. As a penalty for his misdeed, he was sentenced to sixty years in prison and ordered to pay a $120,000 fine. Thanks to EFF's lawyers, Craig was free again: the appeal lasted four days before a Chicago federal court threw out the case.

Very quickly, the EFF and another association called the Computer Professionals for Social Responsibility (CPSR) had established a liberal front against those attempting to police the flow of electrons. Their battlefield was the Net, and the Constitution of the United States was their greatest weapon. They brandished the First Amendment as both shield and sword: "Congress shall make no law . . . abridging the freedom of speech, or of the press; or the right of the people peaceably to assemble, and to petition the government for a redress of grievances."

The Fourth Amendment is their ultimate protection, specifying that no warrants for search and seizure will be issued without probable cause, including a clear statement of what is expected to be seized and where. However prevalent the confiscation of computers and hard disks containing gigabytes of information had become, not to mention the frequency of eavesdropping on telephone and on online conversations, the EFF and its associates deemed these acts to be clear violations of the rights of Americans.

The EFF's lawyers used guerrilla tactics that produced stunning results, invoking the Freedom of Information Act to access any government information relating directly to suspects under investigation. From the first days of the EFF's founding, their initiatives made clear that for several years the federal intelligence services had been spying on the production of servers accessible by the Internet. This revelation served as a wake-up call to cyberspace.

The Clipper Chip and the Attack
on Personal Freedoms

Many of the most vociferous adherents of law and order are suspicious of the Internet. That cyberspace has already become a forum in which people have gathered to meet and get to know each other, or even that an increasing number of economic transactions are taking place there is beside the point. It seems too uncontrollable, too anarchistic, too technological, too innovative, and too full of possibility to be on the level. The police cannot legally monitor and punish deviants on the Net.

As a result, even the police are exploring the new frontier, by trying to pave over it with roadways designed to circumscribe the movements of netsurfers everywhere. The very idea that electronic communications are going unmonitored is an unbearable fact of current law enforcement life. There is no small irony in the frustration felt by law enforcement personnel who, in our democratic societies of the West, see themselves as being stymied by fellow citizens' desires for the sort of privacy one would expect in such a society. This irony is lost on police logic: their desire is to serve and protect, and to do so they will use any necessary means.

In the United States and abroad, there is a long history of the long arm of law enforcement: letters we leave at the post office have been opened illegally before reaching their destinations; phone calls we place have been open to the ears of the officially curious. Such illegal endeavors have largely gone unpunished: they are very difficult to trace and nearly impossible to prove.

For those who would prefer to forget that these sorts of things go on every day in democracies around the globe, there is a vivid reminder in the case of Spanish wiretaps revealed in spring of 1995: their secret services had illegally listened to the cellular phones of various personalities, including King Juan Carlos himself![5] Of course, CESID, Spain's defense information center (Centro Superior de Information de la Defensa), had acted beyond its legal parameters, but such supralegal maneuvers have long been the unofficial norm.

Bad ideas often need little help to succeed, proliferating like bacteria in a petri dish. Former president George Bush endorsed an execrable proposal put to him by the NSA that would add a device called the clipper chip to every telephone or computer manufactured in the United States. The chip would allow authorities to more easily listen in and intercept private communications. Once Bush left office, Clinton embraced the idea.

The idea behind the clipper chip is very simple. Technological progress and illegal eavesdropping are making it more and more difficult for two individuals to have a private conversation. In response, more citizens have begun coding their conversations and messages. Cryptology for the common man (discussed in Chapter 3) then makes it more difficult for law enforcement to do its job—to access the information needed by prosecutors when cases of real illegality arise. And so in 1987, at the urging of the National Institute of Standards and Technology (NIST), and within the scope of project Capstone of the Computer Security Act, the NSA conceived top-secret policing solutions to their new surveillance problems.

Encryption would remain a right of private users for communication via telephone, computer, or fax. And while in the past such encryption would have been made possible by software programs, the new, governmentally conceived method would involve a new piece of hardware added to the guts of computers and telephones, a microprocessor devoted to the encryption of communications. There would only be one model of microprocessor, and it would increase the cost of the devices in which it would be installed by around a thousand dollars. The makers of this clipper chip (whose specifications would remain secret) would be government contractors (VLSU and Mycotronx) who frequently do work for the Pentagon. They would sell the chip to hardware manufacturers, and thus consumers or companies would, for a price, then gain the ability to communicate freely without worry of intrusion or interception.

However, the NSA had an ace up their secret sleeves. Every device outfitted with the miraculous clipper chip would come factory installed with two code keys. These two keys, which make up part of the key escrow system, would reside not only in the buyer's shiny new device but also, in duplicate, on the key chains of two separate, independent entities (which the government never clearly identified) that would have filed the keys according to the key escrow system. These entities could make their keys available in one instance: an investigation of the key's owners for criminal wrongdoing. Were the keys needed for such an investigation, a rigorous procedure for release of the keys would be followed. [6]

The Clinton administration announced this initiative on April 16, 1993, and news of it hit cyber-space like a 100-megaton explosion. That the clipper chip had been the baby of the NSA was par for the course, as far as users in the Internet community were concerned. But when the administration guaranteed that the two keys would remain safe, secure, and well beyond reach of the secret services, that went well beyond what most could stomach. It didn't help that the NSA had sketched the whole scheme in only the broadest of strokes, or that they were planning on running the clipper chip with a new piece of software called Skipjack, all the specifications of which were top secret. Unlike PGP, an encryption program discussed in the next chapter, whose specs are all publicly available and therefore can be dissected by independent analysts searching for possible weaknesses, Skipjack wasn't going to be made available for such scrutiny. This led many to suspect that the NSA would have no trouble breaking it like any of the others it had already authorized for commercial sale, all of which could be considered more or less useless to consumers in search of privacy, since they are easily transparent to the NSA's supercomputers.

This large-scale enterprise against free and private communication was clear as day to those on watch: the NSA and its engineers had been secretly working for four years with manufacturers and the administration before the White House announcement, and production contracts with manufacturers had all been signed in secret a year before. A sarcastic laugh spread across the Net when the administration confirmed that the NSA had verified that no backdoor access into clipper chip was possible without judicial authorization. The day of the official announcement of this initiative marks the first day of the first cyberwar.

The First Cyberwar

The news spread across cyberspace like wildfire, thanks to the work of activists from the Electronic Frontier Foundation. For them there was little doubt that the clipper chip put communication at risk for everyone. The general outcry against the initiative was unprecedented. A petition against the presidential initiative circulated on the Internet and quickly gathered thousands of signatures, among them many well-known names, including all of the network's founding fathers.

Those who opposed the clipper chip were concerned about two issues. Placing the code keys with entities officially independent from the government seemed utterly preposterous. No serious guarantee of secrecy could be believed, and few believed that the keys wouldn't find their way into the hands of the secret services. Although these were far from the most strident criticisms of the initiative, they were the most frequently repeated. Others objected to the uncertainties surrounding Skipjack, an utterly unknown quantity, while still others felt that the microprocessor responsible for this supposed security was outmoded and would prove frustratingly slow.

The coalition opposing this innovation was the largest the Net had ever assembled: it comprised "ordinary" users of the Net, as well as all the subversive elements traveling the Net—hackers and others falling under the general heading of "cyberpunks," including the "cryptoanarchists" and "cypherpunks," all of whom saw clipper chip billowing before them like a red cape. But they were not alone. Computer manufacturers were not pleased to see the government trying to impose inflexible, expensive cryptosystems that would displease their clients, particularly since PGP, which is more flexible, stronger, and more secure, is still available and free. They also weren't happy about exporting products to foreign buyers who would perhaps not be pleased to have the American government holding keys to their information. So the coalition formed. When *Time* magazine[7] polled Americans to see where they stood on clipper chip (many of those polled were still unclear about it), 70% said that it was more important to them to have their privacy protected than to give law enforcement the means of intercepting criminal communications.

Paradoxically, the Internet provided a forum for a new kind of interaction between secret services and activists. Newsgroups contained lively discussions between those for and against, but the talk didn't stop there: negotiations between the two sides took place face to face and toe to toe. This adult interaction, unfettered by the customary respective paranoia and distrust, made several startling encounters possible, particularly that of February 2, 1994, between representatives of the EFF and delegations from the NSA and FBI. A lengthy report of the meeting was circulated over the Net, in which the defenders of free communication were apprised of the particulars of the NSA's demands as well as details of its key concern—procedures for code recov-

ery in clipper-chipped devices. Ingeniously, representatives of the secret services made it clear that
they would not need a judicial order to claim keys,
but would instead fill out a form guaranteeing that
they had legal authorization to do so, which *a pos-
teriori* would be provided. None of this seemed particularly reprehensible to the enforcers of law and
order since, as they claimed, they were only trying
to nab bad Americans, those who would have been
tempted to use encrypted communications for sin-
ister ends.

In the end, even this radical departure from existing laws—a departure that would allow search
and seizure without legal or judicial justification before the fact—didn't make much difference. During
the debate throughout the Internet community, one
of the popes of cyberspace noted: "Under some
vaguely defined and surely mutable legal authority,
they also would be able to listen to our calls and read
our e-mail without having to do any backyard
rewiring. They wouldn't need any permission at all
to monitor overseas calls. If there's going to be a
fight, I'd rather it be with this government than the
one we'd likely face on that hard day. Hey, I've never been a paranoid before. It's always seemed to me
that most governments are too incompetent to keep
a good plot strung together all the way from coffee
break to quitting time. But I am now very nervous
about the government of the United States of America."[8] Journalist Brock N. Meeks added: "Balance,
yes. Total abrogation of my rights? Fat chance."[9]

Since the world had so suddenly changed, anything became possible. So it came to pass that the
bible of netsurfers, *Wired* magazine, one of the most

inventive and original publications on the planet, invited the NSA to contribute an article at the height of the debate. The NSA's chief counsel, Stewart A. Baker, was given three full pages in which to explain the secret services' points of view; there was also a full-page photo of the author in white shirt, tie, and receding hairline. Beginning his article with a comic bow to Jane Metcalfe, *Wired*'s publisher, who had opened her pages to him "with all the enthusiasm of Baptist ministers turning their Sunday pulpits over to the Devil,"[10] the NSA's representative did his best to counter the "myths" surrounding the clipper chip. Of course, Baker claimed that the NSA's only interest was in chasing criminals, stopping "predators" from benefiting from the unfair advantage that inviolable cryptology softwares offer "romantic high-tech anarchism": "We can't afford as a society to protect pedophiles and criminals today just to keep alive the far-fetched notion that some future tyrant will be brought down by guerrillas wearing bandoleers and pocket protectors and sending PGP-encrypted messages to each other across cyberspace."[11]

The idea of these criminals abandoning illegal but highly effective means of clandestine communication in favor of expensive telephones and computers designed to rob them of their privacy seems improbable at least. Furthermore, it is not a little arrogant to believe that all individuals would willingly cede their right to privacy for the sake of supposedly improved law enforcement. As some criminals live in apartments, shouldn't all citizens drop off copies of their keys when they run errands in the neighborhood, with the guarantee that no one would visit them while they were out . . . except with permission from a judge? Nonetheless, despite the number of murders caused by firearms each year, the right to bear arms remains unassailable, whereas the right to have a private conversation has come under the gun.

But the arguments surrounding this issue are of less interest than the reality they hide. For years the secret services have violated the privacy of citizens without the backing of any judicial authority. And while the pedophiles and drug traffickers have been used as an excuse for secret service intrusiveness, the agencies are really interested in keeping tabs on society as a whole—including politicians, artists, journalists, and businesspersons—not simply its malefactors. Although the administration asserted that use of the clipper chip would be entirely voluntary, no one believed it. In fact, a few years later, on August 16, 1995, the Electronic Privacy Information Center revealed the existence of a secret document penned by the FBI, the NSA, and the Justice Department and sent to the National Security Council in February 1993 that spelled out their plans: they wanted anyone intending to encrypt communication to use the clipper chip. By playing up the contradictions swimming around the initiative's eager promoters, EFF activists managed to sink the clipper chip.

On July 20, 1994, in a letter addressed to Maria Cantwell, a congressperson opposed to the NSA initiative, Vice President Al Gore announced that the White House was giving in to the clipper chip's opponents. They weren't abandoning the idea of the clipper chip, but they were asserting that the chip

would no longer be mandatory. In fact, only the administration itself uses the clipper chip, and thus
the device has had a use history about as exciting
as a new copy machine. Does this mean that everyone's privacy problems are over? Absolutely not. It's
one thing to have a public pronouncement of a return to the rights of citizens to communicate freely
in private and commercial life. It's entirely another
to believe that the glory days of cyberspace will flow
gently toward eternity. An attempt at regulating the
ever-increasing electron flow is bound to return,
repackaged more attractively, designed to somehow
harness the ever-growing cybersphere. In a long report tackling the issue, a few government officials
more reasonable and realistic than NSA herald
Stewart A. Baker noted in September 1994, a few
days after the death of the clipper chip: "Concern
over the implications of privacy and security policies
dominated by national-security objectives has
grown dramatically in business and academic communities that produce or use information safeguards, as well as among the general public. . . .
Previously, control of the availability and use of
cryptography was presented as a national-security
issue focused outward, with the intention of maintaining a U.S. technological lead, compared with
other countries. Now, with an increasing domestic
policy focus on crime and terrorism, the availability
and use of cryptography has also come into promi-
nence as a domestic-security, law-enforcement issue. More widespread foreign use of cryptography—
including use by terrorists and developing countries
—makes U.S. signals intelligence more difficult.
Within the United States, cryptography is increas-

ingly being portrayed as a threat to domestic security (public safety) and a barrier to law enforcement if it is readily available for use by terrorists or criminals. There is also growing recognition of the potential misuses of cryptography, such as by disgruntled employees as a means to sabotage an employer's databases. . . . The use of excellent cryptographic products by the myriad array of criminals and terrorists poses an extremely serious threat to the public safety and national security. The essence of the cryptographic threat is that high-grade and user-friendly encryption products can seriously hinder law enforcement and counter-intelligence agencies in their ability to conduct electronic surveillance that is often necessary to carrying out their statutorily based missions and responsibilities."[12]

It would be difficult to set the stakes more clearly. The EFF very quickly understood that though they had won the battle, the government was far from ready to cede the terrain they were fighting on. Reprisals were sure to be brutal.

Though beaten in the clipper chip battle, the NSA and the FBI won an unexpected victory in October 1994 with the Digital Telephone Bill. The bill stipulates that companies setting up digital telephone networks, typically difficult to tap, must make doors into the networks available to the government agencies, so that they can listen in. So while the clipper chip initiative failed to pass whole, pieces of it are making their way into law.

In the United States, as elsewhere, rapid leaps in communications technology have left the police scrambling to take advantage of them and not to be taken advantage by them. Their world has changed;

police must now be concerned not simply with phone conversation but with communication via the Internet. Maintaining a means of access into the ever-broadening range of communicational possibilities is no longer as simple as running a wiretap. The police are as interested in accessing sources of information in homes and businesses as they are in breaking the codes that protect them. But the story doesn't end there.

Sex and Cybercops

The most recent political initiative against the Net, the Communications Decency Act, was launched by Senator James J. Exon (D) and Senator Slade Gorton (R). The act looks to extend the reach of the Federal Communications Commission (FCC) beyond the domains of radio and television and into the brave new world of cyberspace, protecting websurfers against the propagation of indecency, obscenity, harassment, and attacks on personal liberty. The act, an amendment to the Telecommunications Bill, makes content providers, and the networks through which such content flows (for example, phone companies, Internet companies, BBS businesses (Bulletin Board Systems), Compuserve, America Online, and Prodigy), liable for indecent materials.

Officially, this deeply restrictive legislation gives law enforcement officials a means of watching and nabbing possible pornographers, pedophiles, bestialists, scatophagists, and other fetishists that are proliferating over the networks, however discreetly.

For those with a burning interest in bestiality or the very latest in S & M, the Internet is the perfect place to dig deep. But why stop there? The Internet offers free housing to all comers: revisionists and neo-Nazis; partisans of torture and the death penalty; Christian extremists, Islamic fundamentalists; militia members of all stripes; and other perverse paranoids. They all have newsgroups devoted to their interests just as do those who breed hamsters or cultivate roses. After the Oklahoma City bombing on April 19, 1995, even the least experienced websurfer could stumble onto newsgroups containing deranged experts proclaiming that the explosion hadn't been a real success—after all, only 168 were dead and more than 500 wounded; to ensure a more catastrophic blast, they provided bomb recipes and various specifications to such insane ends.

But above all, the Internet is used to send e-mail, adding to textual and scientific archives, facilitating electronic conferences and conversations, and creating newsgroups that aren't always moderated by organizers. Why is the federal government trying to limit the rights of citizens to gather electronically and speak with whom they wish? Because more and more often, children are going on-line, respond supporters of the Decency Act, and something must be done to keep kids from clicking their little mice onto unsuitable material, as well as to protect them from being approached by the electronic equivalent of the shady character on the streetcorner. But where should the line be drawn? In July 1994, a Tennessee jury convicted a young Milpitas, California, couple, Robert and Carleen Thomas, of having sold pornographic photos through the intermediary of their BBS, Amateur Action. The problem becomes clear when we learn that, although the storage of such images on their BBS's hard drive in California was perfectly legal, the retrieval of such images, in Tennessee, was not. And although the Tennesseans who downloaded and paid for the images did so of their own volition, local law sought out and punished the Thomases. Such was the long arm of the law.[13]

Along with other organizations, the EFF has fought vigorously against the return of obscurantism in the form of the Decency Act. One of its organizers, David Johnson, explained on the EFF's website on February 10, 1995, that "We believe policy makers should take into account the ability of those using the Net to avoid materials they find offensive. There will likely be increased use of labels and headers to help people avoid unwanted materials and guide their children's use of the Net in the future. Meanwhile, it is simply a bad idea to make it a crime to 'transmit' offensive material, especially when the 'transmitter' is passive and not monitoring the content of 'transmission.'" Which could nonetheless be seen as part of the problem.

Jerry Berman, of the Center for Democracy and Technology, has attempted to organize opposition to the act, and he believes that any attempt at regulation of the Net is an attack on fundamental democratic freedoms. The Internet, he believes, is able to regulate itself: "Government regulation of content in the mass media has always been considered essential to protect children from access to sexually explicit material, and to prevent unwitting listeners/viewers from being exposed to material that might be considered extremely distasteful. The choice to protect children has historically been made at the expense of the First Amendment ban on government censorship. As Congress moves to regulate new interactive media, it is essential that it understand that interactive media is different than mass media. The power and flexibility of interactive media offers a unique opportunity to enable parents to control what content their kids have access to, and leave the flow of information free for those adults who want it. Government control regulation is simply not needed to achieve the desired purpose."[14] This position has been approved and defended by most organizations fighting for the protection of civil liberties, many newspapers, manufacturers (Apple Computer, for example), and others.

While the battle rages, the network itself has worked out its own solutions to the underlying problems. The stakes are high, since the industries and users most involved with the Net want to keep government regulation as far away as possible and are striving to conduct online business and pleasure according to unwritten rules, using technical tools to help control real problems posed by unfettered electronic liberty. In this spirit, a series of conventions known as the PICS (Platform for Internet Content Selection) was published. The conventions make it possible for adults to program their family browsers to ignore content with rating unsuitable for children. The Recreational Software Advisory Council has been very active in rating software suitability. Many companies are marketing software designed to control access to the Net. They all work along the same lines: each includes lists of sites, periodically updated, to which the software prohibits access. However, these lists are secret and closely guarded by each developer of blocking software. Users don't know precisely what is being blocked, particularly given the number of new sites that proliferate every day. It seems that censorship has reared its ugly head once again, now under a colorful flag raised against "pornography" that is foisting a new moral intransigence on the public. The Cybersitter scandal offers a good example of the risks involved.

Created by the owner of Solid Oak Software[15] Brian Milburn, Cybersitter is part of the new family of blocking software. Like its cousins Netnanny,[16] Surfwatch (made by Spyglass),[17] and Cyberpatrol (Microsystems Software),[18] Cybersitter is to be used to "protect children." But isn't quite that simple. In the online magazine *Cyberwire Dispatch*,[19] Declan McCullagh and Brock Meeks unveiled a few of the secrets behind the development of these blocking programs. Their discoveries are staggering, as they explain that these blocking programs don't merely prevent access to newsgroups and sites devoted to pornography: "There's a darker side. A close look at the actual range of sites blocked by these apps shows they go far beyond just restricting pornography. Indeed, some programs ban access to newsgroups discussing gay and lesbian issues or topics such as feminism. Entire 'domains' are restricted, such as *HotWired*, the electronic edition of *Wired* magazine. Even a web site dedicated to the safe use of fireworks is blocked."[20]

The fun for those who devote themselves to censorship is the daily discovery of new sites they can condemn and prohibit. And when journalists like McCullagh and Meeks began writing about the activities of censors, the censors—whose very livelihoods were now at risk—struck back. Brian Millburn sent the article's authors a threatening e-mail just days after the article appeared: "Your publishing of portions of our copyrighted and encrypted filter file has created problems. The portions you published were source code fragments that give our competitors insight into how our filtering engine works, thus devaluing our product. . . . we will seek felony criminal prosecution under [17 USCS sect 503(a)] of the Copyright Act, and are preparing documentation to submit with the criminal complaint to FBI."

Along with blocking sites like "gay and lesbian rights," "national organization of women," homosexual discussion groups, and feminist discussion groups, Cybersitter censors sites that dare discuss censorship or take issue with the use of blocking programs, much to the great satisfaction of groups such as Focus on the Family, which suggest the program to its members. Those who create and manage banned sites aren't even warned that they have been cyberblacklisted: the banners act with impunity and dubious legality. Discussion groups as minimally menacing to the mental health of minors as alt. feminism, alt.feminism.individualism, soc.feminism, clari.news.women, soc.support.pregnancy.loss, alt. homosexual.lesbian, and soc.support.fat-acceptance are all banned by Netnanny. Those defenders of truth, justice, and cyberspace who have entered into the vault of prohibited words sought out by these programs have found an anthology of supposedly suspect terms that boggles the mind. It is instructive to see what has befallen those who have made such attempts. Jonathan Wallace, who heads the electronic magazine *Ethical Spectacle*,[21] has had some interesting experiences. After denouncing the misdeeds of Cybersitter, *Ethical Spectacle* was blocked. A similar fate befell Benett Haselton, a student and creator of the site Peacefire of the Teen Net Anti-censorship Alliance.[22] Media 3 Technologies, the provider through which the Teen Net Alliance has Internet access, was approached by Millburn, who wanted Media 3 to dump the troublemakers. They refused; Millburn struck back: he blocked not only Peacefire but every site carried by Media 3 Technologies. Glen Roberts has a similar story; his site and the domain ripco.com were condemned. Clearly, moral order and free speech make bad bedfellows.

The Exon Amendment, voted on July 14, 1995, and ratified in February 1996 in a version "amended to a lesser state of absurdity,"[23] still requires that providers do nothing less than closely monitor all e-mail and content that passes through their networks. It stipulates that any provider whether "by means of telephone or telecommunications device, makes, transmits, or otherwise makes available (directly or by recording device) any indecent communication for commercial purposes which is available to any person under the age of 18 years of age or to any other person without that person's consent, regardless of whether the maker of such communication placed the call or initiated the communication" will be liable for prosecution, fines of up to $100,000, and two years in prison.

And so the liberty of the Net—total, limitless, uncontrollable, and often irresponsible—suffered a serious blow during the summer of 1995. Many groups stepped in to prove this point, to prove that the Communications Decency Act was an illegal legislative infringement upon First Amendment rights to free speech. In the weeks following the vote, suits were filed in federal court in Philadelphia by the Citizens Internet Empowerment Coalition, a group comprising Internet providers, libraries, publishers, newspapers, entertainment companies,[24] and fifty-five thousand individuals, working in conjunction with the American Civil Liberties Union. This suit has since become a case study for law schools, under the name *ACLU v. Reno* after Clinton's attorney general Janet Reno.

The judges who first studied the case—Chief Justice Dolores K. Sloviter, Judge Stewart Dalzell, and Judge Ronald J. Buckwalters—probably had little idea how happy they would soon make cyberspace. In their decision of June 11, 1996, they deemed the Communications Decency Act unconstitutional, basing their legal logic on two convergent lines of reasoning. The first, according to counsel for the EFF, asserts that any transmission of ideas "must be treated more or less like the traditional press, and thus deserving of the highest level of constitutional protection, which is referred to in a sort of constitutional-lawyer shorthand as 'strict scrutiny.'"[25] The second argument, counsel explains, rests on a 1949 decision by former Supreme Court Justice Robert Jackson: "The moving picture screen, the radio, the newspaper, the handbill, the sound truck and the street corner orator have differing natures, values, abuses, and danger. Each . . . is a law unto itself."[26]

Judge Dalzell articulated the reasons for his judgment in favor of the plaintiffs in the case: "It is no exaggeration to conclude that the Internet has achieved, and continues to achieve, the most participatory marketplace of mass speech that this country—and indeed the world—has yet seen. The plaintiffs in these actions correctly describe the 'democratizing' effects of Internet communication: individual citizens of limited means can speak to a worldwide audience on issues of concern to them."[27] The Philadelphia judges spoke in no uncertain terms: not only should the Internet remain untrammeled, but any defining of parameters of suitability for Internet content should reside wholly with parents, not the government. The judges found the Communication Decency Act's attempt at muzzling free speech on the Internet was unacceptable and inadmissible: "Indeed, the Government's asserted 'failure' of the Internet rests on the implicit premise that too much speech occurs in that medium, and that speech there is too available to the participants. This is exactly the benefit of Internet communication, however. The Government, therefore, implicitly asks this court to limit both the amount of speech on the Internet and the availability of that speech. This argument is profoundly repugnant to First Amendment principles."[28]

Three weeks later, on July 29, 1996, three Manhattan federal court judges confirmed the decision, declaring the Communications Decency Act unconstitutional. Nonetheless, the blocking software was still available, inexpensive, and efficient. And despite the verdicts, President Clinton had no desire to change his mind. With the 1996 electoral campaign in full swing, he wasn't about to offend conservative voters. In a statement issued shortly after the Philadelphia federal court decision, Clinton stuck to his guns and continued to support the Communications Decency Act: "I remain convinced, as I was when I signed the bill, that our Constitution allows us to help parents by enforcing this Act to prevent children from being exposed to objectionable material transmitted though computer networks. I will continue to do everything I can in my Administration to give families every available tool to protect their children from these materials. For example, we vigorously support the development and widespread availability of products that allow both parents and schools to block objectionable materials from reaching computers that children use. And we also support the industry's accelerating efforts to rate Internet sites so that they are compatible with these blocking techniques."[29]

On December 6, 1996, the Supreme Court decided to consider an appeal by the federal government against the Philadelphia decision. In a justice department brief of January 21, 1997, the government states: "Parents and their children have a First Amendment right to receive information and acquire knowledge, and the Internet has unmatched potential to facilitate that interest. Much of the Internet's potential as an educational and informational resource will be wasted, however, if people are unwilling to avail themselves of its benefits because they do not want their children harmed by exposure to patently offensive sexually explicit material. The government therefore not only has an especially strong interest in protecting children from patently offensive material on the Internet, it has an equally compelling interest in furthering the First Amendment interest of all Americans to use what has become an unparalleled educational resource. The

Communications Decency Act of 1996 constitution-
ally advances those interests."[30] The same day a
coalition of conservative groups[31] announced its
support of the government's efforts: "Sexually explicit material on the Internet poses a unique danger to children, demanding an innovative response
from Congress. In its prior decisions, this Court has
confirmed Congress's authority to address compelling concerns by enacting laws adapting the application of the Free Speech Clause in a novel communications medium. The Internet's capacity to
collect information from numberless sources en-
ables children to view endless amounts of sexually
explicit material without leaving home." On March
19, 1997, lawyers from both parties presented their
arguments before the court.

On June 26, 1997, by a vote of seven to two, the
U.S. Supreme Court dealt the final blow to the Communications Decency Act, affirming the principles of
the First Amendment. It declared that speech must
be as free on the Internet as in newspapers. In the
majority opinion, Justice John Paul Stevens wrote,
"As a matter of constitutional tradition, in the ab-
sence of evidence to the contrary, we presume that
governmental regulation of the content of speech is
more likely to interfere with the free exchange of
ideas than to encourage it. The interest in encouraging freedom of expression in a democratic society
outweighs any theoretical but unproven benefit of
censorship." Within a half an hour after the judgment was handed down it was circulated over the
Net. President Clinton, who had signed the CDA into
law, had this reaction: "We can and must develop a
solution for the Internet that is as powerful for the

computer as the V-Chip will be for the television, and that protects children in ways that are consistent with America's free speech values. With the right technology and rating systems we can help ensure that our children don't end up in the red light districts of cyberspace."

Less than a week later, however, on July 1st, Bill Clinton capitalized on the Supreme Court decision to take a position that will pave the way for the Internet to grow to adulthood. He made this declaration on the occasion of the appearance of Ira Magaziner's report, *A Framework for Global Electronic Commerce*,[32] which insisted on the necessity of leaving the private sector free to develop the Internet "The Internet has such an explosive potential for prosperity, it should be a global free trade zone. It should be a place where government makes every effort, first, not to stand in the way, to do no harm. We want to encourage the private sector to regulate itself as much as possible. We want to encourage all nations to refrain from imposing discriminatory taxes, tariffs or a cumbersome bureaucracy . . . Where government involvement is necessary, it should be to support a predictable, consistent legal environment for transactions."

It is clear that with these two declarations, in keeping with the traditions of the Internet and the well-understood self-interest of its users, the Supreme Court and the President have reinvigorated the American domination of the network. Dynamic, rich, powerful, and now free of internal legal restrictions, American Internet developers have the means to implement these principles of freedom throughout the world. What could stand in their way?

3
Cryptology, Island of Liberty

Since time immemorial, humankind has done whatever it can to keep its communications confidential: different civilizations have created numerous encryption systems to allow their militaries, governments, and spies to restrict acess to their their messages, reaching an apogee of Babel-like perfection with the German Enigma machine, patented in 1919, and immediately put into use by the Kaiser's secret service.

Twenty years after its introduction and just before the Second World War was to explode, the Allies had begun to obtain, via human means, a few pieces of interesting information about Enigma: French counterespionage agents turned over a Nazi dignitary who had given them the first pieces of the puzzle. The Enigma machine was built around three rotors, and then after 1938 around five, allowing for the transformation of one letter of the alphabet into another letter. But the German technicians were able to achieve such a high degree of complexity that Polish mathematicians who, before the war, were able to decode Enigma messages no longer could rely upon the information coming to them from the French Secret Service.[1]

From Enigma to Pretty Good Privacy (PGP)

But to break the integrity of these codes and to discover the principals behind their operation, the work of a brilliant group of mathematicians was required. Led by Alan Turing, the Government Code and Cipher School (GCCS) of Bletchey Park, near London, learned to read Enigma messages as easily as an open book. From the beginning of the Second World War, Turing devoted his energies to cryptology, working on a machine able to generate automatically all the possible combinations that could break Enigma. In order to fully appreciate the effort involved, it helps to know that it was for precisely this application that electronic calculators were invented, thus earning Alan Turing the distinction of being the father of modern computers.[2] In 1946, ENIAC (Electronic Numerator Integrator Analyzer) was installed at the University of Aberdeen by a group led by J. Prosper Eckert and John W. Mauchly, in which Turing did not participate. As the war ended, so too did funding for many of these projects, so work on ENIAC ground to a halt. John von Neumann, a brilliant Hungarian mathematician who was part of the team that built the first atomic bomb,[3] continued to make theoretical progress and conceived a new machine inspired by Turing's ideas, the architecture of which he proposed in 1944 and called Electronic Discrete Variable Computer (ED-VAC). After the war, Turing worked relentlessly with

Max Neuman's[4] team to develop the Mark 1 in Manchester, England, which was completed in 1948. This machine may truly be called the first computer: it had a large memory, could execute a preinstalled program, and used an internal central processor.[5]

Indisputably, the enormous efforts that had gone into making and breaking Enigma had strongly assisted in the birth of computer science. In fact, the work undertaken on Enigma had been so colossal that many of the discoveries made during the operation remained strictly classified and inaccessible for more than half a century.[6] Rumors circulated that during the Second World War, British code breakers had learned that the Reich planned to bomb Coventry, but did nothing to alert those living there, for fear that the Germans would then know that the British had broken Enigma, accusations denied by the British (twelve hundred people were killed in the bombings and sixty-eight thousand buildings were destroyed on August 17 and November 14–15, 1940, and April 8 and 10, 1941). In fact, between June and December 1940, Turing and his team had decoded only five messages generated by the Enigma model they were using. When the battleship *Bismark* left Kiel on May 19, 1941, it took three days to decode the chief officer's message. It was during the summer of 1941 that Enigma messages began to be decoded with great regularity.

The dawning of computer science in the postwar period allowed cryptology to progress by leaps and bounds, by creating more and more complex "keys" to safeguard information and by giving code breakers computational means of breaking down increasingly impenetrable barriers. Essentially, they would proceed by trial and error, arriving at what kind of code was being employed, and then they would plug in every conceivable combination. In fact, these means were little different from how children encode their messages, replacing one letter by another. For anyone who knew the key, reading the message was child's play: direct substitution yields the message. Therefore, one of the weakest aspects of such a system was the need for the encrypter to send to the decipherer the method of encryption.

All the world's information services spend time and money trying to break the numbers that allow embassies to communicate clandestinely with their governments. This is one of the chief functions of the NSA, which has a much larger budget than the CIA and employs almost all of America's ablest mathematicians, most of whom spend their whole careers working for the government. Computer science, just as in its beginnings, remains intimately linked with code breaking, a calculation-intensive endeavor. The French are also intimately involved in code breaking; the entire basement of the DGSE's Parisian headquarters is filled with Cray computers, some of the most powerful in the world. Like its American counterpart, the DGSE recruits the country's top mathematicians and has them work at the central office or at the Centre d'électronique de l'armement (CELAR) in Bruz, near Rennes.

All of these experts are adept at an art which has multiple dimensions. The code systems they create are called *ciphers*, a generic term designating codes and numbers of all kinds. Cryptography is the science of creating and manipulating these ciphers. Those who break the codes, the number crunchers, are encryption analysts. Cryptology is the union of cryptography and encryption analysis. Encryption, by means of a code or cipher, allows for a normal text to be translated into a coded, or ciphered, text.[7] Today, codes are no longer simple systems involving the replacement of one letter by another, or, as in the excellent book by John Le Carré, *A Perfect Spy*, the use of two copies of the same book in which words and letters have been underlined.

Public Keys . . . Secret Keys

A modern encryption system uses a series of very complex algorithms for encryption, and although powerful computers must be used to crack the secrets behind the codes, patience, luck, and perseverance are often the most valuable tools in the arsenal.

One of the most popular encryption systems used in the United States, especially for financial transactions, is called DES, or Data Encryption Standard. It was first authorized for use in 1976 by NIST, the National Institute of Standards and Technology (then called the National Bureau of Standards). DES was approved and is used for commercial applications and "sensitive but unclassified" government use, but not for truly classified work. Originally called Lucifer and invented by IBM, in conjunction with the National Security Agency, this encryption scheme was downgraded in protective strength and today uses encryption keys consisting of fifty-six bits. Each key is composed of eighty seven-bit bytes or computer characters.

DES is flexible and many different versions have been employed throughout the years. Although the security and strength of DES has weakened over time due to Moore's Law (where the power of computing doubles every eighteen months), DES seems to have multiple lives. It's latest iteration is Triple-DES, where two or three cryptographic keys are used in combination to make any attack against a secret message many orders of magnitude more difficult. But, let amateur cryptologists be warned: in the United States, as elsewhere in the world, a government sanction of a particular system of encoding is an *ipso facto* statement that the government has the means in its possession to break it.

Naturally, the best codes are those which the secret services reserve for their own use, and they are never commercialized. All systems of communication between spies and their employers that we know of, no matter where or when they occurred, have had some sort of secret key: text A transformed into text B by secret key C. Whoever has the key can change A to B and B to A. The ideal decoding scenario is to have both texts A and B, from which the key can be deduced. What makes this sort of system vulnerable is that the secret key, in some way, must be sent to the receiver.

In May 1975, the old school of cryptology had its swan song when two researchers at Stanford University, Whitfield Diffie and Martin Hellman, invented a new way of coding messages. The real cryptology nut, Diffie, then only thirty-one, had gotten into math when he was a kid and grew up to be a big shot at Sun Microsystems. The system he and Hellman created made the exchange of a secret key unnecessary.

Imagine that Jack wants to have a private talk with Jill. First, Jack makes two keys: one is private, the other public. He keeps the private key and posts the public key somewhere on the network. Jill, who wants to send Jack a secret message, finds his public key in an online electronic library that anyone can access, and she encrypts her message with it: his key converts her file to gibberish, which she sends along to Jack. Anyone intercepting it will find a coded message without any key to its encryption. Even Jill can't read it. But Jack can. When he gets the message, he takes out his private key and unlocks the message. Conversely, if Jack wants to write Jill , he only needs to find *her* public key and encrypt *his* file with it, for her eyes and key only, a key she keeps on diskette, in her house, in her safe, etc. Thus, no more worries over managing the secret keys: everybody has one, close at hand.

Back when the Internet was taking its first baby steps, the principle behind this public key system heralded major advances. Then, only government agencies were using the codes, and barely managing it at that; now, a broad cross section of users seems to have caught on. In fact, the idea and use of public keys constituted an unprecedented advance. Not only could coded messages be sent without the worry of interception by cybercops or nosy hackers, but public keys allowed the authentication of messages, ensuring that the sender was who he claimed to be.

One of the first public-keyed encryption systems to compete with DES was developed in 1977 by three MIT researchers (Ron Rivest, Adi Shamir, and Leonard Adelman) and launched as RSA. Soon the most well informed coders were combining the two as a means of redoubling their security. For example, Jack starts by encoding his message with DES by means of a secret key. Next, using Jill's public key, he encodes the DES key. Jill, upon receipt of Jack's message, reprocesses the DES key before decoding the message with her personal key.

Although other public systems have been developed since RSA, it has become something of a norm for the most sophisticated of American governmental systems. Not only does RSA safeguard the nuclear launch codes of the U.S. arsenal, but, remarkably, it protects the Russian launch codes as well.

So Why Bother?

If no one ever envisioned a day when average citizens would be able to scramble their telephone conversations, it was only because the fairly basic means to such an end did not exist, or else were being reserved by virtue of draconian legislation for use by highly placed public officials, the police, or the military. But things changed in the beginning of 1995 when the program Nautilus was launched, thus transforming the computer into an inviolable telephone.

The telephone is a disarmingly hardy means of communication whose rudimentary technology allows only voice transmission (sometimes not very well), but offers the undeniable advantage of being used all over the world. To communicate by voice alone, however, is now considered insufficient. In the age of the Internet, an ordinary microcomputer and a cheap modem can use those old copper wires to great advantage, sending gigabytes of information and e-mail of all kinds across the globe for the cost of a local phone call.

But there, of course, is the rub: digitization of communications is a godsend for Big Brothers everywhere. Whether they tap into phone lines, to satellite transmissions, or, even better, to an Internet node, the electronic nature of these messages means that the unmarked van parked in a dark alley, filled with surveillance equipment and highly trained listeners, is a thing of the past. The observers no longer have to physically listen in: they can simply snatch up the bits of information off the supply lines and filter them down to the coded bit of gold they contain. Essentially, intrusion has reached its own sort of industrial revolution. No longer is there any sort of guarantee, real or imagined, that someone isn't listening. Regardless of the rules or restrictions governing the actions of the secret services *vis-à-vis* citizens' individual liberties, taps of all kinds are so easy to set up that they'll probably be used more often now, not less, by official information services and private agencies. All international communication is monitored randomly, but monitored nonetheless. The world champions of this game divide their efforts fairly evenly between obscurantist totalitarian regimes and the great democratic nations.

It is clear that in the name of defending the hon-

or of democracy the police of the world lose no sleep in violating the individual liberties of private citizens and, today, are insinuating themselves into the information networks, just as they had into telephone lines. When asked, they all justify their actions in the same way: they're just using the means at their disposal to stop the flow of drugs, major theft, and spies of all stripes. To get hold of these bad guys, they assert the need to legitimately penetrate the intimacy of the majority of the population. Laws protecting private life, of which the inviolability of one's home is a basic tenet, also guarantee the judicial branch of government the right to carry out searches, but only after they have been judged evidentiary clear and necessary, and after the citizen under scrutiny has access to some sort of legal aid, no matter how basic. And if this is true for normal means of communication, so it should be for cyberspace.

Whether you like it or not, if you want to avoid having your communications intercepted on the Internet, there's really only one solution: encode them. This is the only way to deter members of secret services, administrators of the networks, and assorted hackers from stealing their way into our private lives. Of course, some coding systems are better than others, and with cryptography, as with everything else, you get what you pay for. And there isn't much likelihood that most of us would want to invest the kind of money necessary to have our own little Enigma on a shelf in the den next to the Sony Play Station and the VCR.

But with the introduction of the encryption system PGP, which allows for a quasi-certainty of inviolability, this may all have changed. The scope of

this revolution may be measured in the degree of up-
set in which the secret services now find themselves
as they scramble to regroup. A barrier seems to have
been erected, a siege wall protecting the privacy of
the masses.

Let There Be PGP

The effectiveness of PGP is due to its successful
combination of three other systems: RSA, IDEA, and
MD5. And despite the modesty of its inventor, who
likes to say that his software offers "pretty good" privacy, the program has become the international
standard in a matter of months, much to the cha-
grin of the Orwellian observers.

But PGP would not have been such a bright idea
had there not been another IDEA first. The International Data Encryption Algorithm (IDEA) was
launched in 1990 in Zurich, Switzerland, by James
L. Massey and Xuejia Lai, and because of it's innovative approach to encoding, texts now encoded with
PGP—even identical texts encoded with identical
keys—never look the same twice. IDEA translates
the message as a whole, using a key of 128 bits;[8] for
all sorts of civil researchers, breaking IDEA has become their favorite game. They haven't succeded nor
have their counterparts in the intelligence services
(although if they had, they wouldn't brag about it).

Imagine, theoretically, that a microprocessor
could calculate so fast that it could verify one million different keys per second. Now imagine that one
billion of these microprocessors were simultaneously devoted to doing just that. It would take 10 billion

years to try all the possible permutations of 128 bits. While the speed of computers continues to increase and their cost decrease at a very rapid pace, it will probably never get to the point that IDEA could be broken by the brute force attack. The only type of attack that might succeed is one that tries to solve the problem from a mathematical standpoint by analyzing the transformations that take place between plain text blocks, and their cipher text equivalents. IDEA is still a fairly new algorithm, and work still needs to be done on it as it relates to complexity theory, but so far, it appears that there is no algorithm much better suited to solving an IDEA cipher than the brute force attack, which we have already shown is unworkable. The nonlinear transformation that takes place in IDEA puts it in a class of extremely difficult to solve mathematical problems.[9]

The most recent versions of PGP (MIT 2.6.2, Viacrypt 2.7.1) continue to use, in addition to IDEA, RSA's concept of "asymmetrical ciphering," which handles keys of up to 1,024 bits (308 digits, indeed 2,048 bits). The probability that a direct attack against such a key would ever be successful is nonexistent. If it would take 10 billion years to make a successful direct attack on a code keyed with 128 bits, a code keyed with 2,048 bits would take 10 billion to the fifth power, a number 259 digits long.[10] But of course, cryptological connoisseurs know that you don't attack asymmetrical systems directly.[11] The best way—the mathematicians out there will appreciate this—is to factor a number that is the same length as the key. A team of sixteen hundred researchers worked for more than a year in 1994, using thousands of microcomputers scattered across

the globe, linked via the Internet, before they succeeded at factoring a number 129 digits long. It
might be worthwhile to mention that anyone using
keys made up of more than 128 bits is more than
just a little bit paranoid. With this sort of paranoia
common to those trusting their documents to PGP,
it must be most reassuring for them to hear that the
system's promoters commonly recommend the use
of keys made up of 512 bits (154 digits).

Bruce Schneier has figured out that it cost
$10 million to arrive at this number.[12] Estimating
that by 2010 the cost of computer-science-based
information will have been lowered significantly,
such an operation will only cost about ten thousand
dollars; *but* it will still cost you *$3 million billion*
($3,000,000,000,000,000) to break a key with 308
digits. All of this theorizing has brought about in-
numerable quarrels in certain circles and has made
others realize that just as our current computer
technologies were born out of the need to break
Enigma so too will future generations of computers
be born that will hobble RSA and PGP.

It should be abundantly clear that the difficulties of code breaking become nonexistent if you can
get hold of someone's personal key. Therefore, the secret services, by doing what they are already good
at—breaking into peoples' houses and all the variations thereof—can simplify things dramatically. Protecting one's password has become the number one
priority for those who use PGP. Phil Zimmerman has
thought very carefully about this and has outlined
precisely what one should do to safeguard one's key:
"To protect your secret key, you can start by always
keeping physical control of your secret key. Keeping

it on your personal computer at home is OK, or keep it in your notebook computer that you can carry with you. You should only use your secret key on a machine that you have physical control over. Don't store your pass phrase anywhere on the computer that has your secret key file. Storing both the secret key and the pass phrase on the same computer is as dangerous as keeping your PIN in the same wallet as your Automatic Teller Machine bank card. It would be most secure if you just memorize your pass phrase and don't store it anywhere but your brain. If you feel you must write down your pass phrase, keep it well protected, perhaps even more well protected than the secret key file. . . . No data security system is impenetrable. PGP can be circumvented in a variety of ways. In any data security system, you have to ask yourself if the information you are trying to protect is more valuable to your attacker than the cost of the attack. This should lead you to protecting yourself from the cheapest attacks, while not worrying about the more expensive attacks. Some of the discussion that follows may seem unduly paranoid, but such an attitude is appropriate for a reasonable discussion of vulnerability issues."[13] Good advice from Uncle Phil.

Various means are available for hiding these bulky numerical keys—long strings of characters that defy memorization—other than, say, writing them on big Post-It notes stuck to your monitor. One way involves using a smart floppy diskette. Though externally indistinguishable from a standard 3.5 floppy, its insides contain microprocessors and interfaces that communicate directly with the heads of the diskette reader. This little diskette generates the public and private keys randomly, but only the public key will be known by the user; the private key remains secret even to the user. A copy of the diskette can be made, and losing it would definitely not be in one's best interests.

PGP and the Internet

Phil Zimmerman is a radical from way back. Protests against nuclear power twice landed him in jail. Though now a computer analyst, he's still a militant pacifist. Bringing together his professional abilities with his political convictions and his fascination with cryptography, he set out to adapt RSA's public key system—which hitherto had been so complex as to only make it practical on big, costly computer systems—for use with personal computers. Though he conceived the notion in 1977, the project didn't take over his life until 1984, by which time he was working day and night. He was so possessed he often forgot to pay his bills and almost lost his Boulder, Colorado, house. But it wasn't until 1991 that he finally created a product he was satisfied with. He would write a few years later, "PGP also has far-reaching political implications. Mostly good ones. In the Information Age, cryptography affects the power relationship between government and its people. The Government knows this all too well, as evidenced by their recent policy initiatives for the Clipper chip, which would give the Government a back door into all our private communications—an Orwellian 'wiretap chip' built into all our telephones, fax machines and computer networks. PGP strikes a blow against such dark trends, and has become a crystal nucleus for the growth of the Crypto Revolution, a new political movement for privacy and civil liberties in the Information Age. This government has done all they can to stop the emergence of a worldwide encryption standard that they don't have a back door into."[14] All it could do, but to no avail. Because PGP did just that.

As soon as he had finished and tested the first version of his program (which at the time only worked on a PC format), Zimmerman rejected the idea of selling it and instead did what any good computer scientist would do with software he wanted to see reach everyone: a friend of his posted it on a BBS (Bulletin Board System) from which it could be downloaded via the Internet free of charge. Within a few hours on one day in June 1991, PGP was downloaded into thousands of computers across the country. A few days later, the author began to receive e-mail from around the globe.

Zimerman's haste in making it available, after so many years of careful preparation, was not accidental. He had heard that a bill was before the Senate trying to limit the general public's access to cryptography, and he realized that PGP would stop it in its tracks.

Though he had worked like a maniac to perfect his program, Zimmerman hadn't troubled very much over the details, some of which presented problems: although he used part of RSA to make his own software work, he had neglected to request permission from its rightful owner. After a lot of legal back and forth and sizable financial threats, in September 1993, Zimmerman made a deal with the holder of the commercial license for RSA, Viacrypt.

After his legal problems were over, Zimmerman devoted himself to business. According to *Forbes* magazine, he raised no less than eight million dollars in 1996,[15] that not only allowed him to create his firm Pretty Good Privacy, Inc., in January of 1996, but to buy out Viacrypt in July of the same year. Zimmerman, formerly chairman of the board and CEO, then brought in Dr. Thomas Steding, ex-president of Novell, Inc., as president and CEO of the firm, which by 1997 employed forty programmers. Today, PGP is having offspring, and the family is preparing to grow even further. Just think of all those people who are ready to spend $149 to buy PGP. Those who use Windows 3, DOS, MacIntosh, and UNIX have PGPmail. Those with Windows 95/NT can get PGPmail 4.5, as well as PGPcookie cutter that insures security for web use. They can all get PGP-phone, an encryption software for telephone communications. PGP also exists as freeware (PGP 2.6.2 and PGPphone 1.0), accessible on the MIT site at http://web.mit.edu/network/pgp.html, with the co-operation of PGP, Inc. Note, however, that international acquisition by non-U.S. citizens of commercial products, as well as those from MIT, is prohibited.

Saint Zimmerman, Cybermartyr

All these various commercial vicissitudes were finally straightened out by businesspeople acting in good faith who were just as eager to sell a means of communicating in perfect secrecy to the netsurfing public. But unhappy Philip Zimmerman had swum out into dangerous waters, where he crossed an opponent more troublesome than the business world sharks: the U.S. government.

In the domain of cryptology, the NSA had been the be-all and end-all until the invention of public keys and Zimmerman had exploded unexpectedly onto the scene. For decades, the NSA had been using cryptology unimpeded. As the NSA devoted an important part of its energies to breaking the codes used in diplomatic transmissions, it didn't want to have to worry about American codes. American encryption systems such as DES were already in the NSA's sights—and if they didn't yet have the key, they could break in with a toothpick—despite IBM's statements to the contrary. As John Perry Barlow puts it: "The encryption watchdog is the NSA. It has been enforcing a policy, neither debated nor even admitted to, which holds that if a device or program contains an encryption scheme which the NSA cannot break fairly easily, it will not be licensed for international sale. Aside from marveling at the silliness of trying to embargo algorithms, a practice about as pragmatic as restricting the export of wind, I didn't pay much attention to the implications of NSA encryption policies."[17]

There are a few good examples of cooperation between big business and the NSA: the encryption system used by the American cellular phone network is "transparent" for the secret services, as well as various "export" versions of software with passwords that are alarmingly breakable. The NSA even forbade IBM to install a cryptography microprocessor in their AS/390.[18]

The arrival of PGP shocked the NSA with all the force of a high-tension wire, and it decided to fight back. But just as the Constitution protects freedom of speech, it gives Americans the right to encode their communications. The fact that Zimmerman hadn't respected rules to a game that the NSA had decided unilaterally didn't change anything: whether revolutionary or not, whether the NSA could break PGP or not, Zimmerman was protected by the First Amendment. From that point of view, the NSA didn't have a case against him.

So they went after him from another angle. Although the link between the Puzzle Palace and the case that was launched against Zimmerman has never been proven, Zimmerman was taken to court. A judge in San Jose, California, launched the attacks indirectly. He decided that Zimmerman could be tried for the illegal exportation of arms, as defined by ITAR (International Traffic in Arms Regulations). The only encryption systems ITAR approves for export are weak as kittens, with keys that don't exceed forty bits; and ITAR's official stance is dictated directly by the NSA's interests. If PGP is in circulation abroad, huge amounts of information relating to U.S. national security will be indecipherable to the NSA.

It's a strong argument that has been the subject of fiery debates. In a *Wired* article that greatly contributed to the general awareness of radical cryptographers, Dorothy Denning, a leading expert at Georgetown University, stated: "If we fail to enact legislation that will ensure a continued capability for court-ordered electronic surveillance, systems fielded without an adequate provision for court-ordered intercepts would become sanctuaries for criminality wherein Organized Crime leaders, drug dealers, terrorists, and other criminals could conspire and act with impunity. Eventually, we could find ourselves with an increase in major crimes against society, a greatly diminished capacity to fight them, and no timely solution."[18] Donn Parker, an expert on computer science information, adds: "We have the capability of 100-percent privacy. But if we use this I don't think society can survive." In a parody of NRA language Barlow responds: "You can have my encryption algorithm . . . when you pry my cold dead fingers from my private key."[19]

The debate has grown so intense that a new breed of radicals has been born, cypherpunks. Their art is to write encryption programs that will ensure inviolable private communications. Their charter explains: "Cypherpunks assume privacy is a good thing and wish there were more of it. Cypherpunks acknowledge that those who want privacy must create it for themselves and not expect governments, corporations, or other large, faceless organizations to grant them privacy out of beneficence. Cypherpunks know that people have been creating their own privacy for centuries with whispers, envelopes, closed doors, and couriers. Cypherpunks do not seek to prevent other people from speaking about their experiences or their opinions. . . ."[20]

He wants to improve PGP and write a version that will permit encryption of telephone conversations. Nonetheless, he feels that the tool he has developed, for all its qualities, both good and bad, now belongs to the public: "I don't like to see criminals use this technology. If I had invented an automobile, and was told that criminals used it to rob banks, I would feel bad, too. But most people agree the benefits to society that come from automobiles—taking the kids to school, grocery shopping and such—outweigh their drawbacks."[21] An argument which the cryptoanarchists are pushing to the limit.

Cryptoanarchists go one step further. They aren't afraid of using provocation in the name of unbridled liberty. They traffic recipes for making bombs, and they often pick fights directly with the federal government. The *Crypto-anarchist Manifesto*, available over the Internet, was written by Timothy May, a former Intel employee who retired at thirty with spectacular stock options. His intentions are utterly unambiguous, and he advocates cryptology as a means of achieving total liberty: " . . . The State will of course try to slow or halt the spread of this technology, citing national security concerns, use of the technology by drug dealers and tax evaders, and fears of societal disintegration. Many of these concerns will be valid; crypto anarchy will allow national secrets to be traded freely and will allow illicit and stolen materials to be traded. An anonymous computerized market will even make possible abhorrent markets for assassinations and extortion. Various criminal and foreign elements will be active users of CryptoNet. But this will not halt the spread of crypto anarchy. Just as the technology of printing altered and reduced the power of medieval guilds and the social power structure, so too will cryptologic methods fundamentally alter the nature of corporations and of government interference in economic transactions. Combined with emerging information markets, crypto anarchy will create a liquid market for any and all material which can be put into words and pictures. And just as a seemingly minor invention like barbed wire made possible the fencing-off of vast ranches and farms, thus altering forever the concepts of land and property rights in the frontier West, so too will the seemingly minor discovery out of an arcane branch of mathematics come to be the wire clippers which dismantle the barbed wire around intellectual property. Arise, you have nothing to lose but your barbed wire fences!"[22]

This wild ideology has some perverse side effects. It allows American right-wing militias to keep their communications confidential, and bomb recipes as well as racist theories and other bits of of triumphant, extremist rot to be easily passed around. Whatever they may say or write on the Net, the cryptoanarchists are no different from those trigger-happy extremists trying to eliminate the federal government or the United Nations (considered by some to be the embryo of a world government), all of it seasoned with undisguised anti-Semitic bile.

It seemed Zimmerman would become a thorn in the U.S. government's side, a martyr to the cause of cyberliberty, a symbol of the larger need for privacy, and as symbol bear the brunt of the fierce legal dealings. But on January 8, 1996, his lawyer Phil Dubois received, to his great surprise, a fax from the assistant U.S. attorney for the Northern District of California, William Keane, informing him that his client "will not be prosecuted in connection with the posting to USENET in June 1991 of the encryption program Pretty Good Privacy. The investigation is closed." The press release of the same day said: "No further comment will be made on the reasons for declination." News of this decision, made after the California attorney had consulted with the Department of Justice, spread like wildfire through cyber-space. Tens of thousands of users of the program throughout the world applauded. And the solidarity among users all over the Net, who went so far as to create a legal defense fund to pay the lawyers working on the case,[23] clearly paid off. Mike Godwin, lawyer for the Electronic Frontier Foundation, which supported Zimmerman throughout the affair, declared after the decision: "It is a real black eye for the government. They wanted to be very proactive in chilling the distribution of encryption technology on the Net. It backfired. What it did was entrench a lot of people against the government policy."[24]

The defenders of the rights of man in cyber-space—believing that the right of one and all to encrypt communications is the best means to prevent intrusion into one's private life—weren't the only people in Zimmerman's corner. Many companies joined in the outcry against the legal proceedings. American industrialists and businesspersons, all of whom were within their legal rights to use the software within the United States, risked putting themselves in an awkward position with respect to the ITAR law every time they left the country with the program on the hard drive of a laptop. Nonetheless, no one would deny the need of such an individual to communicate with the home office privately and safely. So with the necessity for encryption understood and accepted as a *sine qua non,* the U.S. government found itself up against industrialists who had no intention of limiting themselves to a choice between plague—temporary export of cryptology software in violation of U.S. law—and cholera—traveling the world with computers, programs, and files perfectly transparent to anyone who might want to peek. Because the keys that the U.S. government had authorized for international use were only forty bits, which are notoriously weak, on August 16, 1995, a young Frenchman succeeded in breaking a key that protected the leading Internet browser, Netscape. A month earlier, a group of cryptology experts had responded to a challenge to break the key put to them by the cypherpunks. Damien Doligez, twenty-seven years old, was the first to succeed in a few hours one weekend, using 112 personal computers linked at the Rocquencourt research center belonging to INRIA, France's national institute for computer and electronic research. Another team, with members around the world linked via the Internet (including Adam Black in England, David Byers in Sweden, and Eric Young in Australia), had done the same thing two hours before him. So, if a good computer scientist with good hardware could manage it, what self-respecting, ramtoting hacker wouldn't be able to do the same thing? Damien Doligez made clear the risks in a statement after his successful gambit: "Someone who uses a credit card to purchase something over the Internet is at risk of having that number nabbed by a pirate up to no good but his own."

The weaknesses of many cryptosystems can in part be traced to the penchant mathematicians have for breaking them for scientific fun. On April 10, 1996, a scientific team led by Arjen K. Lenstra[25] of Bellcore announced that they had succeeded at factoring the code RSA-130,[26] further reinforcing the idea that longer codes are necessary to keep communication confidential. PGP, which uses very long keys, is safe from these sorts of misfortunes. The conclusion to draw from these incidents is that if the U.S. government is willing to approve the general use of forty-bit keys, they must have no difficulty breaking them. And if they propose to raise the limit to fifty-six bits, as they did in October 1996, the story is still the same On this very point, an article was published by a group of high-level scientists, on the occasion of Dr. Matthew Blaze's speech to the U.S. Senate Commerce Committee, Subcommittee of Science, Technology and Space, on June 26, 1996: "Fortunately, the cost of very strong encryption is not significantly greater than that of weak encryption. Therefore, to provide adequate protection against the most serious threats—well founded commercial enterprises or government intelligence agencies—keys used to protect data today should be at least 75 bits long. To protect information adequately for the next twenty years in the face of expected advances in computing power, keys in newly deployed systems should be at least 90 bits long."[27]

The great paradox in the fight waged by governments against cryptology for everyone, symbolized by PGP, is that the executive powers are more than aware that control can rest with the state and that an evolution in legislation is indispensable. Without it, they'd have to kiss good-bye any hope of network surveillance, which you can bet is not a part of their plans. As Europe begins to regain its footing in cryptography, the United States, since the abandonment of the clipper chip, has been trying to build legislation it can live with, which will impose limits on all individual users and on all businesses. The main idea behind any and all such efforts is unchanged:

they want all users of cryptological software to make their secret keys available, one way or another, to authorized holders to which police and information services would have access. On August 17, 1995, Ray Kammer, associate director of NIST, revealed during a colloquium of the Software Publishers Association that the government would soon allow the export of encryption programs as powerful as those used on U.S. soil. The conditions are still strict, since "the encryption products [must] remain in the possession of the exporting person or the possession of any another citizen or lawful permanent resident traveling with him/her, are for their exclusive use and not for copying, demonstration, marketing, sale, re-export or transfer of ownership or control." Which is a step in the right direction. But this still doesn't fly in the face of the needs of the secret services. Louis Freeh, director of the FBI, made his position perfectly clear before the International Cryptographic Institute on September 21, 1995: "In order to do all of the things we want to do in public safety—as well as in commerce and for national security—we must be strong proponents for encryption. But, what we think needs to remain the same is the lawful court-authorized access that we have enjoyed for more than a quarter of a century to the conversations, the records, the plans of those who would break our laws, whether they be terrorists, organized criminals, nuclear smugglers, drug traffickers, or spies."

What is the solution? Early in 1996 the United States continued to refine its position. The National Research Council released an enormous and remarkable study on the subject which recommended not legislating against the exportation of cryptology systems, since they are already widely available across the world.[28] One interesting sideline to the nearly open dialogue on cryptology in the United States is the impact it's having on Europe. France, formerly a leader in this domain, along with many other European countries, is beginning to adopt positions very much in line with those of the United States. On May 20, 1996, Bruce W. McConnell and Edward J. Appel, co-chairs of the Interagency Working Group on Cryptography Policy, made public a report on the subject commissioned by the White House.[29] Based on the principle that had won the rejection of the clipper chip, this study proposes the institution of a public and private key management organization called Key Management Infrastructure (KMI). Each user would deliver a set of public and private keys, guaranteed by a certificate authority. An escrow authority would be responsible for keeping the secret keys and would only give them to the police in the event of an investigation of the keyholder and after the justice department had issued its okay. Attorney General Janet Reno addressed the issue one month later, but without much of a clarification of how KMI would work and who would be running it. For Reno, there is only one real issue: "The consequences of the spread of unbreakable encryption would, in fact, have far broader impact because we would also lose our ability to search for and seize stored data and other forms of electronic evidence. Whereas we might be able to get a regular search warrant if we had encrypted data, that search warrant would be of no use unless we had the key."[30] The Internet community's response to this unambiguous position has been the same as those leveled during the clipper chip debate: privacy is privacy, whether for individual or the commercial user, and no one wants to give it up. Still during the summer of 1996, as pressure rose on both sides of the fence, Marc Rotenberg, director of the Electronic Privacy Information Center (EPIC) of Washington, DC, and a faculty member at Georgetown University Law Center, burned through a speech before the Senate that accused the administration of trying to breathe new life into the clipper chip through the key escrow scheme: "Users did not simply object to the proposal that the government will hold the keys, they objected to a technology that was clearly intended to promote government and surveillance of private communication."[31] According to EPIC, which shares this opinion with other defenders of privacy on the Net, what matters to the U.S. government is that its secret services retain the same unfettered access to electronic communication that they currently have with telephonic communication. Rotenberg continues: "It is a critical to understand that the White House continues to believe that encryption should only be available if it can easily be broken. There have been several proposals all based on this same premise. Each has a new name. The White House will promote 'Voluntary Key Escrow.' They will endorse 'Commercial Key Escrow.' They will support 'Escrow Encryption Standard.' And they will back a new plan for 'Key Management Infrastructure.' Call it what you will, it is still Clipper."

During the 1996 elections, the question of privacy on the Internet became a part of the debate. Republican senator Conrad Burns of Montana chose his warhorse by getting together with conservative colleagues Larry Pressler of South Dakota and Robert Dole, then a candidate for the presidency, as well as with Democrats Patty Murray of Washington state and Ron Wyden of Oregon. The original clipper chip proposal was made during the Bush administration by the NSA and the FBI and was endorsed by the Clinton administration. Today, EPIC finds big advantages to the proposition "Pro-CODE" (S.1726) put forward by Conrad Burns, who proposes to confer control over the export of cryptology programs not to the NSA or to the State Department but to the Commerce Department. A press release on the EPIC website claims the bill has three main principles going for it: "1) prohibiting the government from imposing government-designed encryption standards on the private sector. 2) prohibiting "big brother" from mandating a back door into people's computer systems. 3) updating US export controls on the sale of encryption products in foreign commerce, and placing US businesses on a level playing field with their foreign competitor." On July 12, 1996, the White House officially announced its new position, coming out against Pro-CODE: "the bill is unbalanced, and makes no effort to take into account the serious consequences of the proliferation it would permit." According to the text, "a consensus is emerging around the vision of a global cryptography system that permits the use of any encryption method the user chooses, with a stored key to unlock it when necessary. The encryption key would be provided voluntarily by a computer user to a trusted party who holds it in safe keeping."[32] Candidate

Dole quickly attacked his adversary: "President Clinton has championed a key escrow scheme in which the use of strong encryption is only permitted if the key, or password, is made available to the government, brings back memories of the administration's failed bureaucratic, complicated, and unworkable health plan."

Cryptology: A World Defiant

All U.S. commercial Internet interests agree that their supremacy in the world of information is now at stake. Since these companies represent the driving force behind and within the Internet—its creativity and its software—they can't understand why the government wants to put a wrench in their gears. Microsoft, Netscape, Lotus, and others find it intolerable that they should have to downgrade the quality of their cryptology modules to comply with U.S. export laws, in so doing put their livelihoods and those of their customers at risk. The government and the companies do see eye to eye on one point: for whatever reason (Zimmerman!) both now agree that cryptology is no longer solely the government's domain. Spies, diplomats, and military personnel are no longer the only users of cryptology, and history isn't about to move backwards, however much the government might prefer it to. And it is precisely for this reason that the NSA lost its cool. Millions of free copies of PGP are in circulation, and the world is a different place for it. Nonetheless, the United States is the only country where such a distribution is legal. Everywhere else, particularly Old

Europe where state traditions are slow to evolve, cryptology remains a taboo subject. The European states, whether independently or as a part of the European Union, have a certain view of history in their minds when they think about cryptology. Of course, PGP has spread across the continent, whether due to jurisprudential vagueness or in direct violation of applicable laws, as in France.

Strong anticryptology legislation has been passed in Paris, no doubt due to the military's deepening involvement in cryptology. Before 1986, French legislation was perfectly clear: cryptology was a weapon of war. Nearly no exportation was allowed, and the use of any sort of cryptology on home soil was strictly prohibited. Using a cryptosystem would have been as difficult as taking a tank out for a spin around the block. In February 1986, then prime minister Laurent Fabius made a first attempt at less restrictive legislation a few weeks before his parliamentary majority was overturned by legislative elections, leading to his replacement by opposition leader Jacques Chirac. This decree, prepared by the SGDN (Secretary General of the National Defense),[33] changed little on the surface but created a specialized structure designed to lead France into the cyberage: DISSI[34] (Interministry Delegation of Information Systems Security). It was made a part of the military and its functionaries depended, and still do ten years later, on the secret services. French industrialists in the world of high-end banking terminals that use memory cards had great difficulty during this period exporting their products and protested vigorously against such restrictive legislation. Their protests were heard, and yet another law was adopted in December 1990. It stipulated: "To preserve the national defense and the security of the interior and the security of the State, the furnishing, exportation or use of means of benefiting from cryptology are restricted to: a) preliminary declaration when this means or this benefit can have no other object than to authenticate a communication or to insure the integrity of a transmission; b) a preliminary authorization by the Prime Minister in other instances."[35] Which is to say: if you want to encrypt your signature for an authorization, that's fine, but the rest of the message must remain transparent. This does really represent a step forward, because in the past you weren't even allowed to encrypt for authorization purposes. But if the government position has changed (albeit timidly), it hasn't come as a result of pressure from Netsurfers, who represent less than two and one half percent (2.4%) of the population (150,000 at the end of 1996). It is the industrialists who have been waging a protracted siege for several reasons: they want to be able to safeguard their data, but they also don't like watching the United States gobble up the cryptography market. The French administration finally admitted that the companies were correct, but added one point: according to the SCSSI, programs like PGP are tampered with by the NSA. This was asserted, of course, without any proof. And based on this baseless assertion, the French government decreed that no French company could use PGP, but they could use programs designed in France by companies most often working for the Ministry of the Defense—programs whose effectiveness is, to say the least, less certain.

In June 1996 the French parliament approved a

new telecommunications law which included a notion dear to the U.S. government: "the trusted third party"—a version of key escrow, the phoenix of cyberspace. The French law authorized that from that day forward companies and private citizens could purchase programs from trusted third parties[36]: each buyer would agree, however, that if one day they were to fall afoul of the law, law enforcement would have the right to reclaim the private key from the trusted third party so that police could access the suspect's confidential files. It is highly unlikely that any criminal would submit to this sort of prenuptial agreement. Such individuals would most likely prefer using PGP despite its illegality, leaving the government with the same problem it started with.

As 1996 drew to a close, the world was inching closer to international legislation against cryptography in one form or another. On September 26, 1996, the OECD, which was trying to organize such a legislation, held a meeting in Paris on the subject. A second meeting of the OECD was to occur December 16–20 in Paris. The day before, militants in favor of cryptography staged a countermeeting, in Paris, to reiterate their opposition to desire on the part of the United States, France, and Great Britain to limit liberty. The meeting, keynoted by the Australian judge Norman Reaburn, allowed activists to articulate their positions, among them Whitfield Diffie, Matt Blaze, Philip Zimmerman, and Ross Anderson. Their statements had all the fire of speeches made by generals before going into battle.

During this period, everything seemed to indicate that events were moving into a decisive phase. On October 1–2, the United States opened fire once again, beginning a new chapter in the history of cryptology by confirming reports that an alliance had been forged between the White House and a few of the biggest manufacturers of information-related materials most related to hardware. For Vice President Al Gore, who on the first of October published his statement on the question,[37] it was about promoting "the growth of electronic commerce and robust, secure communications worldwide while protecting the public safety and national security." In short: encryption is good, given certain limits. More precisely: "Under this initiative, the export of fifty-six-bit key length encryption products will be permitted under a general license after one-time review, and contingent upon industry commitments to build and market future products that support key recovery. This policy will apply to hardware and software products. The relaxation of control will last up to two years." Manufacturers must adjust to the new definition of the law and have two years to do so, adapting their products to the standard of the key recovery system as it is put in place. By the end of 1998, the vice president affirms that, "the export of 56-bit products that do not support key recovery will no longer be permitted." And to ensure that key recovery will not go the way of the clipper chip, a promise of dialogue comes with the concept: "The administration will use a formal mechanism to provide industry, users, state and local law enforcement, and other private sector representatives with the opportunity to advise on the future of key recovery. Topics include: evaluating the developing global key recovery architecture; assessing lessons learned from recovery key implementation; advising on technical confidence issues vis-à-vis access to release of keys; addressing interoperability and standards issues; identifying other technical, policy, and program issues for governmental action. The administration is broadly consistent with the recent recommendations of the National Research Council. It also addresses many of the objectives of pending congressional legislation." The day after the announcement, ten American manufacturers[37] and the French national group Bull announced the creation of an alliance "to develop an exportable, worldwide approach to strong encryption. The goal of the alliance is to enable companies to conduct secure international electronic commerce." In reality, the only difference between the key recovery system and key escrow is in a user's ability to find a lost key, while a judiciary decision could also allow law enforcement agencies to recover the key.

The White House outlined many specifics in its brief of October 1, including the information that eventually the keys could be managed from within the user's organization and that a system of international cooperation would allow for the recovery of keys on foreign soil, *a form of cryptographic extradition.* Organizations fighting for civil liberties quickly rose up to fight the new initiative. As of October 3, the Center for Democracy and Technology refused to acknowledge a difference between key escrow and key recovery, arguing that "the attempt to institutionalize key escrow worldwide is a fundamental threat to the privacy and security of Internet users, both domestically and abroad."[38] In a conspicuous editorial, the *New York Times* criticized this new initiative: "There is room to improve the plan. . . .

There is time to work out restrictions, in cooperation with the industry and privacy advocates, for the next generation of encryption software. In the meantime, the administration might push forward on the [NRC] panel's other sensible recommendations, such as developing better encryption expertise within the FBI, and helping the private sector develop the encryption software it needs to stop illegal eavesdropping."[39] The *Washington Post* celebrated the change that had downgraded cryptological software from its former munitions-level status, but wondered what form the key recovery plan would take. "What kind of plan? Nobody can quite say. What if the plans aren't acceptable? Licensing will revert to the old rule in two years. Will the security issue be moot by then? Probably. Barring some burst of clarity, one is left wondering whether the administration has compromised or caved, and what it now believes about the dangers of exporting uncrackable software."[40]

Behind the battle for cryptology a larger war rages. The fight between the supporters of an Orwellian state and the cyberpunks, one hopes, will find some realistic middle ground: something like a cyberdemocracy where the state, in its role as protector of our liberties, will allow citizens to communicate freely, protecting against intrusions into their private lives. All over America, whether on Ruby Ridge or on college campuses, the debate has been exacerbated by the popular belief that the federal government has been interfering too often and too deeply with the lives of private citizens.

4

The Jolly Roger Rides the Net

Anthony-Chris Zboralski is only twenty-two and looks like butter wouldn't melt in his mouth. Tall and slender, with mischievous dark eyes, a tousle of hair, an abrasive sense of humor, and a level-headedness that contasts starkly with his experience, he doesn't seem fazed by the time he's served in prison. He was born in 1975, before personal computers existed. At the age when his contemporaries were glued to television cartoons, he began his adventures. At eight, a little Thomson MO5 computer ran aground at the foot of his Christmas tree, and within a couple of months he was deeply involved in this new technology: by 1983, when France was taking its first steps toward an interactive telephone yellow pages called Minitel, Zboralski was on their trail. But his first serious hacking activities came when he was fourteen. He says with perfect frankness: "I was working on a very theoretical level; telephonic computer-science is like a philosophy. I gave it a lot of thought." Zboralski broke into the the French telephone network, first under the pseudonym Taxman, then Frantic, and became known among the hacker community, starting his own club called

Abuse for his hacker pals. He was perfectly bilingual in French and English and had an unusual talent: he could mimic anyone, French or American, old or young, male or female. When I asked if he used some sort of machine to transform his voice, he said, "I can't. It's too cold. The person on the other end of the line immediately feels ill at ease." In 1992, he ceased to be a good-natured do-it-yourselfer, and his fame extended beyond his intimate circle: he made the Scene. That's what the hackers call their planet.

Hey, Mister: How Do You Become a Hacker?

The Scene is a planet without borders, its members mutants who have evolved with a telephone glued to one ear and a computer keyboard growing out of the tips of their fingers. They open their eyes when most people sleep, and work when the systems operators sign off and most offices close. How many souls populate this little planet? Tens of thousands, of whom perhaps two hundred reign as princes. Most of them are in the United States, others in Germany, the Netherlands, and France. The best Europeans are in Scandinavia. And on September 19, 1996, these Norse hackers hit paydirt: they penetrated the CIA's Web site.[1] It wasn't a matter of interfering with the CIA's secrets held in Langley, Virginia. In accordance with the most basic computer security measures, the CIA's computers aren't connected to any network but their own internal network, so their Web site is completely out of the loop. Sometimes, however, ridicule can cause damage as serious as that of actual violence. In this case, hackers were out to have some fun, to show that with their little keyboards and computers they could be stronger than the richest and most powerful information-gathering organization in the world, and from an ocean away. So the little rascals managed to enter the site and to change how it looked and functioned for those users who visit it—some 120,000 a week who are there to consult the mediocre World Fact Book. In place of the usual message of welcome, the hackers had inserted "Welcome to the Central Stupidity Agency." The photo of then chief John Deutch, who is known for his temper and must have really taken it badly, was replaced by that of an unknown. The links to other services offered by the CIA were replaced by others: "News from Space," "Nude Girls," "Stop Lying," all of which gave links to faraway sites that had much more to do with hacking than they did with American national security. Rick Oborn, one the CIA's spokespersons, willingly admitted that "this is not anything that would cause us great concern." No doubt. But thousands of newspaper articles and television reports carried news of the attack all across the planet.

In the beginning, all hackers went by the nickname "phreaks" or "phreakers," designating those who use their computers to grab access codes from the account managements systems at the heart of big phone company computers, allowing them to make free phone calls. They either remain connected via modem to the same computer, half a world away, or just talk to friends. Interestingly enough, they usually never meet these friends, despite speaking to them at length, several times a day, for years, a virtual club. These phreakers know how to get into the biggest American telephone exchanges, private branch exchanges (PBX), and to do pretty much whatever they want. They can call a particular business number and use it as a relay for another phone call. Traveling businesspeople save huge amounts of money by dialing these numbers, avoiding hotel phone bills; when phreakers get hold of these numbers, they can save even more, at huge cost to companies.

Another lucrative phreaker pastime involves acquiring calling card numbers and passwords set up for consumers by AT&T, Sprint, France Télécom, etc. If a hacker gets a bunch of these, he or she can charge relatively small calls to a variety of cards, on the principal that the charges will go unnoticed. The world record for this little gambit is held by Max Louarn, caught in September 1994 in Majorca, Spain, for having trafficked over 140,000 calling card numbers, sold throughout the United States and across the world by BBS hackers.[2] Often, these cards would be sold to foreign émigrés for around one hundred dollars per week, allowing them unlimited talktime anywhere in the world. The hacker could renew the numbers on a weekly basis, and there was nothing to prevent the buyer from selling the numbers to someone else. While certainly not inexpensive, its cost was a far cry from that of the going legal rate.

To sell these numbers, you have to get them first. So airports are filled with phreakers, haunting the gates and waiting for businesspeople to get off their planes and settle into a phone booth, calling card number in hand. With a trained eye, they read the number as it is punched in, waiting for the caller to add his or her secret code. And then they're gone, back to the keyboard. Even the most watchful can get taken, as Henry M. Kluepfel, a Bell research lab employee, learned a few years ago: "I made a call from a coin phone and shielded the number from the scruffy-looking guy on my left, but I was unaware of the guy in the business suit on my right."[3] The phreakers are organized: in a few minutes, Kluepfel's card was used six hundred times across the United States before Bell's security people got wind of it and canceled the growing catastrophe. How much does telephone fraud of this kind cost its victims? The U.S. Secret Service determined that, in 1994, $2.5 billion of phone fraud was perpetrated. The telecommunications industry estimates between $1 billion and $9 billion.

Zboralski had another bag of tricks: "social engineering," of which he was, he claimed, one of the biggest specialists in the world. He called one business after another and conned the management into giving him the numbers of all the credit cards charged during the day, under the pretext of verifying these accounts as a representative of the credit card network. Then he would use these card numbers to make purchases of computer equipment by telephone. Could he send them a fax confirming his order? No problem, he'd send it along. "Can I send a courier to pick up the stuff?" And then he would go there himself and have them sign a phony invoice.

In January 1994, he had a run-in with the law. He chose his victims carefully: "I even called one of them up to talk to him about it. The guy said I'd run up about two thousand dollars on his card, but that it wasn't a problem. The insurance would cover it. Anyway, I only did it with really big companies." Listening to Zboralski, you'd think anything could be gotten over the telephone: an American Express card number and its PIN; a computer password; a telephone calling card. The only thing more remarkable than what this young hacker could do was how gullible his victims were.

In order for Zboralski and his band to finesse a teleconference of fifteen hackers without paying a penny, they used AT&T's Alliance system, which multinational companies use to talk among themselves. The call will originate in the United States, and they'll dial a number that links all their parties without having a separate charge for each participant but rather one charge paid by the company. Like all telephone listings, many of the numbers are close to other numbers, a digit off here and there, making it easy to find others by a little trial and error.

For Zboralski, calling the United States from France and convincing the machines that the call originated domestically was child's play. Bouncing from switchboard to switchboard, he would find numerous teleconference numbers, one of which turned out to belong to the FBI. Then he called the U.S. embassy in Paris and got the name of the FBI's Parisian counterespionage chief, Thomas Baker. "I said to myself that this was so big that they would never even notice. In fact, they didn't question any of it. When I decide to do something, I'm always certain it's going to work . . . ."[4] Next, he had to pass himself off as Baker to get past "Patricia," one of the secretaries in an American FBI office, in order to get some phone numbers. The FBI finally got wind of the dimensions of Zboralski's success when one day he called, again passing himself off as Baker, who, that day, just happened to be in the adjoining office.

Of course, the whole thing turned out badly. Humiliated, the FBI filed a complaint and estimated that it had lost around $250,000. Zboralski was put in provisional custody on April 10, 1995, or actually, was returned to custody: his fun and games with credit cards had already landed him in jail in Melun, France, and it was here that the gendarmes waited to arrest him again. He got out of jail quickly, but a new trial was waiting for him. On February 25, 1997, he found himself in front of the Twelfth Circuit Court of Paris, where he had to explain to the court how he could have so little "moral sense." His explanations of the computing counter-culture did not persuade the court, which delt severely with him, ordering reimbursement of the monies demanded by the FBI, as well as a suspended sentence. But Anthony has had a change of heart since his run-ins with the law. He has written a book that will come out in the fall of 1997, and he has started, like any self-respecting hacker, his own computer security company, Immunis. Clearly, the prevailing wisdom in the real world holds true on the cyberscene: if you want to protect yourself from break-ins, hire a thief to show you how.

Phreaker, Hacker, Cracker?

Frantic the phreaker is also a hacker and uses the most sophisticated techniques when breaking into remote computers. Though these terms take on slightly different colorations across cyberspace, there are certain recurring themes. Phreakers hack telephone systems: John Draper, best known to his phreaky friends as Captain Crunch, discovered that a 2,600-Hz signal would allow him access to AT&T's internal management computer. Phreakers also figured out how to generate and introduce the exact frequency that a quarter makes when dropped in the slot, allowing them to convince pay phones that they're gorging on quarters. From a technical perspective, telephonic hacking as practiced by phreakers is far more basic than hackers' hacking: if the former is shoplifting sugarless gum, the latter is grand theft auto of a Ferrari. Hackers break into computer systems and usually do it without any malicious intent: they're in it for the sport. Gifted computer science experts with brains that outthink the most complex microprocessors, their kind of fun is penetrating closed systems and browsing their guts, much like a tourist might visit a historic building or museum. And if they happen to take a program or some information along the way, they don't see it as theft so much as sharing—souvenirs from the gift shop.

Often hackers will spelunk into the innermost depths of these giant computers to hide secret servers in regions of the computer that are rarely visited and in which they'll put prohibited information (software used for circumventing safeguards, for example, or servers of pornographic material). By using a part of a university or institutional computer, the hackers have access to far more memory than they could ever afford, and need not put themselves at risk by storing illegal items on their personal hard drives. They can access this material directly by calling it up through a specialized line, since many of these computers aren't hooked up directly to the Internet. Those that are enable, as the FBI confirms, nearly 80% of all hackers' connections.

The meanest of the hackers, often called crackers, try to destroy what they can: erase files, install "logic bombs." And then of course there are the nuts—people who try to sabotage their own company's computers, and so forth.

Recipes and formulas are exchanged, clandestine BBSs proliferate, newsgroups that touch upon or talk directly about the theme of hacking spread across the USENET network.[5] Various highly active mailing lists furnish hackers with the latest news in their field, much like those newsletters received daily by their opponents about them.[6] There are also journals devoted specifically to their interests, such as *Phrack* and *2600*, both available on the Internet. Some of these journals are available at the newsstands or by subscription, but some are only available online, such as *CUD* (*Computer Under-ground Digest*).[7] Hackers aren't merely a bunch of cuddly adolescent thrill seekers. In the United States, a group that calls itself the ILF (Internet Liberation Front), probably an outgrowth of the Masters of Deception or the Legion of Doom, specializes in inundating the electronic mailboxes of those journalists not fortunate enough to have met with their approval with mail bombs or "flames"—vast quantities of lewd, threatening e-mail. Legion of Doom (LoD), one of the most famous groups on the American hacker scene, was founded during the eighties and takes its name from among the cartoon hero

Superman's fiercest enemies; this hacker club had been led by a computer scientist specializing in telecommunications systems who had taken the pseudonym—or in hackerspeak, "handle"—Lex Luthor. Later, Texan Chris Goggans (aka Erik Bloodaxe), along with several LoD members, were investigated by the secret service in 1990, although Goggans and other Texas-based members were never prosecuted.[8] Since its creation the Legion of Doom has become the prime mover on the scene, its members surveying their territories with a savage wit and a technical *savoir faire* that never ceases to amaze their followers at home and abroad and that is ever in evidence on their clandestine bulletin, the *LoD Technical Journal.* At the end of the eighties, LoD quickly became the American reference for information on hacking, so much so that the police responsible for investigating these invisible computer scientists fairly assumed that if anything serious happened across cyberspace, these were the guys responsible. In the years since, hackers have come to occupy a unique place in the American collective consciousness, and while it would be premature to say they have taken on folk hero status, they do embody a sort of *fin de siècle* pioneering ethic in keeping with the romantic ideals upon which the country was founded: "Hackers believe that essential lessons can be learned about the systems—about the world—from taking things apart, seeing how they work, and using this knowledge to create new and even more interesting things. They resent any person, physical barrier, or law that tries to keep them from doing this."[9] Like explorers, they meet their discoveries with great enthusiasm, publishing their findings for the benefit of their equally enthusiastic audience. But loyalties within this community are always changing, and it isn't unusual for war to break out, as it did between the Legion of Doom and the Masters of Deception (MoD).[10] The war was straight out of some medieval fiction, with heroes and villains, lords and vassals, and in the end its victims.[11] Essentially, MoD decided to flex its muscles, and some former LoD members, witnessing the display of vanity, decided to teach them a lesson. It began with MoD planning to attack a computer security company called Comsec, founded by Chris Goggans and two other LoD members in 1991. Goggans and his Comsec partners thought that this was going too far and decided to pursue MoDs and rein them in by setting up a sort of cyberspace neighborhood watch to keep the networks safe. Goggans claims that they gave MoD every chance to tone things down before Comsec sent the evidence they had been collecting to the security service of their telephone company, in addition to the FBI and the Secret Service. MoD has since claimed that Comsec's heroics weren't some valiant species of cyberspace self-policing, but a racially motivated attack (Comsec are southern white males, MoD are largely not). This is difficult to confirm. It has been reported that one day Erik Bloodaxe sent Phiber Optik an ad for Legion of Doom T-shirts. This earned him a death threat in reply, assuring Bloodaxe that the only way he would return from an upcoming computer security conference was in a body bag.[12] The members of the Masters of Deception[13] were accused of some very serious crimes, including eavesdropping on phone conversations from public phone networks, eavesdropping on data transmissions, intercepting data transmissions, owning computer cracking hardware and software equipment, stealing passwords, selling passwords, stealing credit profiles, selling credit profiles, destroying computer systems, and causing losses of $370,000.[14] These young people, who hadn't earned a penny from their hacking mischief except in one incident, were sentenced severely: in 1993, Paul Stira and Elias Ladopoulos spent six months in federal prison and six months in home detention. John Lee was sentenced to a year in jail, three years of supervised release, and two hundred hours of community service. Julio Fernandez agreed to testify against Mark Abene and received a suspended sentence. And Mark Abene, the best of the best, was sentenced to a year in prison.[15]

Chris Goggans is unquestionably one of the most important actors on the hacker scene. He is rumored to have pulled off some spectacular bits of mischief for which he has never been caught. But he is also the respected editor-in-chief of the wildly successful *Phrack*. The magazine has taken on mythic proportions within the hacker community and is the online bible for all the world's computer delinquents. It is the bane of the God-fearing, a vending machine of bomb recipes, tools of the trade, and means of breaking and entering computers far, far away. More than enough to send shivers up the spine of cybercops everywhere, but also a good way of taking the pulse of the scene. Chris Goggans works during the day, and at night, every night, he sets aside an hour to read e-mails from around the globe, "from everywhere there's electricity, from Russia, from Asia, I get e-mail. Six hundred per week . . . ." And of

course his faded jeans, his long hair, and other outward manifestations of counterculture cool have,
with time, evolved. When we met in the fall of 1995,
Goggans had already launched his own computer
security company and was wearing a beautiful suit,
and an immaculate shirt. When he turned around,
of course, his ponytail hanging down to the bottom
of his back gave warning that he hadn't swallowed
the establishment whole. A year later, in the luxuri-
ous sitting room of a Washington, DC, hotel, his
bright eyes were as filled with life as ever, but his
hair was now short.

Good Doctor Goggans has two sides, and he has
hidden one of them. If Mister Bloodaxe is still alive,
he's in another region of his cerebral cortex. At the
end of September 1996, he had just completed Number 48 of *Phrack*. It contained all the expected information on hacker strategies but also his "last" editorial. It was his good-bye to the Scene, and it had
little resemblance to the posture of the erstwhile cy-
berwarrior. Instead, he put forward a point of view
not uncommon among hacking's pioneers, that the
appreciation of the technical complexities of computer systems and the sport of figuring them out
have been lost, and that those cardinal virtues have
become secondary to ignoble ends. So Goggans made
his summing up of what hacking had been and what
it has become in no uncertain terms: "I don't like
most of you people. The hacking subculture has become a mockery of its past self. People might argue
that the community has 'evolved' or 'grown' somehow, but that is utter crap. The community has de-
generated. It has become a media-fueled farce. The
act of intellectual discovery that hacking once rep-

resented has now been replaced by one of greed, self-aggrandizement and misplaced postadolescent angst. . . . It would seem that 'hacking' has become the next logical step for many people looking for an outlet to strike back at 'something.' 'Well, gee, I've already pierced every available piece of skin on my body and dyed my hair blue . . . what on earth can I do now to shock my parents? I know! I'll break some federal laws, and maybe get my name in the paper! THAT WOULD BE COOL! It'll be just like that movie!' I hate to burst everyone's bubble, but you are so fucked up. In this day and age, you really don't have to do anything illegal to be a hacker. It is well within the reach of everyone to learn more, and use more powerful computers legally than any of us from the late 70's and early 80's ever dreamed. Way back then, it was all about learning how to use these crazy things called computers." A few weeks after writing that editorial, Goggans further explained: "Today nobody has to do anything illegal to learn. Period. There was a time in the distant past where the only manner in which to learn was to steal access, but today for free you can download more powerful operating systems to run on your home PC than we ever could fifteen years ago. The need to break-in has been removed. The only reward from breaking in to someone's computer system is from stealing proprietary information or from getting high off of doing something you know was wrong. This is not what hacking was ever about back then, but unfortunately, it seems to be what it is about now. People who engage in this are not 'rebels,' they are mimics, engaging in some high-tech-pantomime whose original meaning has been lost over the ages."

As far as he's concerned, the clash between the "rebel ideology" of the original hackers and that of the new generation shouldn't pose a serious problem to anyone; he, for some time, has been moving down the orderly road that puts America first. And he's not alone on this road, as I was able to observe at a November 1995 meeting of Open Source Solutions[16] organized by Robert Steele; this former CIA and Marine Corps operative was the first to take hackers seriously and to see what they could contribute to the intelligence community. This was an uphill battle, as hackers still struck fear into the hearts of businesspeople everywhere. Steele sees himself as a bridge between the two communities, hacking and information gathering, and on a larger scale, the defense community. Sitting before us on this icy November afternoon was a panel of one the most impressive quartets of hackers the world over (except Kevin Mitnick, who, since the previous February, had been in federal prison in Wake County). Sitting with Chris Goggans was Dark Tangent, known to his friends as Jeff Moss. The hackers surveyed their audience: dozens of captains of American industry, chiefs from the information-gathering community, and other Pentagon high-ups. Gathered together in the Hotel Omni Shoreham in Washington, DC, all the participants were on pins and needles. It would be worthwhile to mention that Dark Tangent is the organizer of the craziest congress the world over: Defcon, a hackers-only convention. On this day in Washington, surrounded by diabolic counterparts, Eric Hughes was in seventh heaven. With red beard and hair even longer than Goggans's, had been Hughes, founder of the cypherpunks, is one of the world's most powerful computer scientists, living a laid-back lifestyle in Berkeley, California. Cyberlibertarians and mathematicians without equal, his disciples fight with him in the name of liberty and unfettered personal freedom over the Internet, and have only two real passions in life: breaking encryption codes in vulnerable systems, and writing code destined to confound government "cryptoanalysts" and make their computers beg for mercy. The panel was completed by black-haired dour Emmanuel Goldstein. He's the head of a magazine for phreakers (telephone hackers) called *2600*.[17] Why this number? Because that was the exact frequency that a quarter made while tumbling into a payphone during the hacking ice age. Captain Crunch, a hacker precursor, had made that little discovery that had allowed pirates to make free phone calls for years.

Why were these hackers present for an information community conference? Primarily to let it be known that they are good boys and good Americans, ready to join the Information War and help prevent the electronic Pearl Harbor[18] that many military officials fear. Robert Steele, the head of the OSS, had briefed the 350 conference participants at the outset: "Yes, we've invited some hackers. They're bearded, they don't wear suits, they never get up before noon. But these are unconventional warriors, and America needs them. Some of them deserve spankings, but they deserve the opportunity to say that the emperor is naked. They are one of our most valuable national resources!" A year later, Steele confirmed his assertions: "I first decided that hackers needed to speak publicly to top government officials when I realized in 1992 . . . that we have a very frag-

ile and easy to destroy communications and computing infrastructure. This information is TOP SE-
CRET in most countries, for a stupid reason—fear.
Hackers are like astronauts, full of the 'right stuff'
and constantly exploring the frontiers of cyberspace—they have much to teach all of us."[19]

But don't old habits die hard? Is the switch from
banditry to patriot games too much to expect? To a
rapt audience, Goggans explained: "Hackers aren't
bandits. They do what they do for fun, not for profit. They want to enter into a system, write, 'I went
this way' on a virtual wall, and then call the administrator. The real hoodlums aren't teenagers anyway. Engineers up on UNIX can do just as well.
That's where you should look for the criminals." In
the conference room, sweat was on every brow. Goggans continued: "The Japanese and the French want
to steal the information in your systems. We hackers could care less. We hackers don't have money.
They do, and with it can buy all the information they
want." But truth be told, Goggans's financial worries
are in the past, now that he's a hired gun: companies pay him to break into their computers and then
plug up the holes he finds. In the room a rubicund
Space Command general raises his hand. "We know
we're vulnerable. What should we do to prevent piracy?" Dark Tangent stares daggers at the general:
"Close everything. Encode everything. Callbacks.
Faxes. Telephones. E-mail. Don't leave anything out
in the open. And using a cellular phone is like giving a speech to a crowd." Goggans broke in: "Close
your electronic doors. Stake out the Internet. Look
outward and inward." The general sat back down,
looking helpless. A businessman asked, "What do

you think of firewalls?"[20] The panelists exchange glances. They break into broad smiles. "Do you make them?" a hacker asks. "No, I have one." "Well, make sure you're using dynamic passwords or phrases.[21] They should be generated arbitrarily and should be constantly changing." In the room, you could hear a pin drop.

Times are changing. The bad guys are now the good guys. But, of course, it isn't quite so simple. Many are against giving hackers too easy a path to respectability. After the Infowar conference of September 1995 in Washington, DC, Donn B. Parker, a computer security consultant, bridled at the idea of hackers being given such a pulpit from which to preach: "Malicious hackers are our enemies and proven criminals or supporters of criminals, not our friends. Wannabes think that if they can do things as outrageous as your friends by attacking information owners and their weak systems, they can also receive your attention. . . . Hacking is a fantasy, short cut route to success that you are creating and encouraging. This means you are luring our young, potential infotechnologists into a degrading, dead-end life of malicious hacking."[22] Peter S. Tippett, President of the NCSA (National Computer Security Association) and co-organizer of the meeting, felt that it was perfectly expected and respectable for hackers to be given a place to speak: "Among other things, the lack of true understanding of the real threat leads to all kinds of misappropriation of resources in corporate information security departments (like worrying about 64-bit versus 128-bit keys while leaving yourself open to all kinds of attacks based on lying, cheating, stealing, conniving, or shared bravado, hacker competition, gang think, and so on). It also leads to all kinds of conjecture, speculation and, yes, even some positive folklore about hackers which is no doubt misguided."[23]

Wherever you come down on this issue, however, the small, powerful class of systems engineers that manages the information networks within large corporations is as yet unable to protect itself against hackers. Such attacks, therefore, mean all-nighters for the computer operators, some of whom even throw together little programs that call them up automatically via their beepers. Attacks on a central computer, whether or not they precede real break-ins, often take advantage of user laziness—an incompatibility between the rigors required of safeguarding systems and the laxity of those charged with the task. One of these vulnerable points is the management of passwords which most often are far too basic, easily arrived at by software designed to generate and plug in possible choices. Other programs exist that are designed to break more complex passwords: Crack, Shrack, Crackerjack, Cracklib, NPasswd, HaughII, etc.

Programs even more powerful exist and are used by various government security services, many of which are produced by the U.S. company Accessdata: WR Pass and MS Word. Security software like COPS and SATAN use such integrated systems, which actually turn out to be quite useful to the hackers, since the code-breaking modules are already integrated into the programs. By inputting the most common words in a language one after another (both proper and common nouns), they're able to gradually nibble away at the computer firewall that is supposed to protect against the hackers' assault.

All self-respecting hackers use password dictionaries now and again,[24] but they can compile them themselves just as easily, using various databases that hold virtual shelves of books, like Gutenberg.[25] None of the hackers we've met thus far has ever been seriously slowed down by a password: if women's names, names of famous streets or cities don't do it, *Webster's* should have every conceivable variant somewhere within. And if the computer rejects them (after three wrong tries the computer will usually disconnect), the hackers' system still automatically calls back, for hours if necessary, until it finds a way in. One technique often employed involves overcoming a series of barriers, firewalls, and dynamic passwords before downloading the password management files of the computers under attack, allowing hackers to crack them at home, taking all the time they wish, and without the risk of being rejected by the machine and being noticed. Given that a good cracker can run about fifty thousand passwords per second past such a management file, it seems that this is the best way to go.

The various creators of sophisticated computer information protections have already come up with a number of commercially available softwares like Firewall 1, Sidewinder, Gauntlet, Raptor, and, the most widely known, BorderWare (which used to be called JANUS).[26] But it seems that these shields do little more than attract the attention of knights with longer, stronger lances. The U.S. military, which for some time has been deeply involved in such matters, believes that the only real solution to the problem of infiltration is the introduction of programs into their systems that track users' movements from the moment they log on. How can they keep hackers from getting in? Perhaps by increasing and heightening the hurdles they'll face, making the most sensitive information accessible only after the most rigorous computer obstacle course conceivable.

SATAN Is Good for You

Hackers can never have too many good things to say about Dan Farmer and Wieste Venoma, the two creators of hacking's most powerful program: SATAN (Security Administrator Tool for Analyzing Networks). SATAN has been known for a couple of years by systems administrators, who have been using it to find the weaknesses in their own systems, the better to protect them. To better illustrate the wholesale perversity that has taken hold of the cyberworld, SATAN's innovation did not begin and end with its technical virtuosity: its distribution across the Internet on April 5, 1995, was undertaken after a major media publicity campaign and ensuing widespread panic, in order that the hackers and those who were protecting against their attacks would be able to enjoy the great satisfaction that apparently comes from meeting on the battlefield equally armed. When he finished perfecting his program, Dan Farmer was still responsible for security at one of California's best known software companies: Silicon Graphics. He had decided to work there rather than the NSA, which had called him about a job that then got caught in a tangle of bureaucracy.

During his free time over three years, Dan Farmer had dreamed of putting together a means by which his colleagues could help safeguard the information of their employers. However, as it evolved, it became clear that with the remarkable graphic interface of his software—very similar to the Mosaic browser created by the NCSA (National Center for Supercomputing Applications)—the ease that it afforded a computing ignoramus and the speed with which it found the weak points in a system also made it the perfect tool for hackers. No longer would they need such high levels of expertise or the costly online time required to sharpen their skills.

Silicon Graphics believed that his product could ruin their reputation. They would have much preferred that it be reserved for exclusive use by those wishing to safeguard the security of their companies, and therefore the company wanted to prohibit it from being distributed across the Net. But this wasn't what the programmer decided, as he made clear in a press conference on March 1, 1995, where he admitted that he was certain, at some point, that SATAN could cause damage. And this is what got him fired, despite his advocacy of responsible use. Farmer also expressed how his choice was consistent with his lifestyle: "I am bisexual. I am into S&M. I'm into security. I'm into good wine. Why should I hide? The whole idea that what is not normal should be kept secret—that's really distasteful to me."[27]

As news stories began to appear, more people learned of SATAN and panic ran rampant throughout cyberspace. How would the doors the programmers had opened be shut? And these remorseless hackers—who had gone where they shouldn't have gone, who had stolen software for the fun of it, who had brought programmers and companies to the brink of disaster—how would they be stopped?

In the face of these computer disasters, the best shields companies can find are, naturally, the hackers who've turned coat. They too make use of specialized Internet newsgroups, exchanging their robbery techniques, trying out various firewalls they've made. If you wanted to subscribe to the mailing lists on these various subjects, you'd receive up to one hundred lengthy e-mail messages per day. Hackers and counter-hackers know each other and fight each other, although they're not always entirely able to tell which side of the line each is on.

Most stunning of all is the speed at which news travels, counterorders are given, and errors are uncovered. Beginning April 5, 1995, CERT (Computer Emergency Response Team) of Carnegie-Mellon University in Pittsburgh—put on its feet by DARPA (the Defense Advanced Research Project Agency) and still funded by the government—has been flooding the network with information generated by COPS (another program by Dan Farmer that can help to combat SATAN's aggressions).[28] And the Lawrence Livermore Laboratory announced the same day that its program COURTNEY does the same job, and that SATAN is available on its server; fifteen hundred copies were made of it immediately.

The conferences where pirates regularly assemble are curious affairs. On June 2, 1995, *Phrack* magazine organized its annual conference, the Summercon, in Atlanta, which would no longer be by invitation and in secret, but open to everyone: "Hackers, Phreaks, Pirates, Virus Writers, System

Administrators, Law Enforcement Officials, Neo-Hippies, Secret Agents, Teachers, Disgruntled Employees, Telco Flunkies, Journalists, New Yorkers, Programmers, Conspiracy Nuts, Musicians and Nudists."[29] The rules of the game, according to the invitation posted on the Internet, are clear: "It has always been our contention that cons are for socializing. 'Secret Hacker Inpho' is never really discussed except in private circles, so the only way anyone is going to get any is to meet new people and take the initiative to start interesting conversations. . . . The formal speaking portion of Summercon will be held on one day, not two or three, leaving plenty of time for people to explore the city, compare hacking techniques, or go trashing and clubbing with their heretofore unseen online companions."[30] Nowadays at meetings of this type it is not unusual to find a mix of hackers, FBI agents, varied Secret Service people, and firewall programmers mingling together.

If You Build It, They Will Come

Kevin Mitnick thought that it would never end. Prince of hackers, he had been haunting the networks with impunity for years. Nothing was secret from him; he could enter any computer. No matter how robust or purportedly impenetrable, he always found a hole in the fence he could squeeze through or an electronic crowbar he could fit to the task, an artist of infotration. But on February 15, 1995, years of smooth sailing quickly collided with choppy seas. The reason was simple: Mitnick couldn't restrain himself.

Was he truly an "information terrorist" as Justice Department spokesman John Russell called him shortly after his arrest? It seems somewhat excessive, Mitnick more resembling a postmodern, high-tech Robin Hood than a mad bomber. Nonetheless, he did some damage during his decade of clandestine activity. Although he was only seventeen in 1981, Mitnick was already being pursued by the authorities. He managed to copy, via computer, key information from Pacific Bell's central computer. He was also one of the first to successfully penetrate NORAD (North American Air Defense Command), the agency that safeguards the airspace over the United States and Canada. This little prank even caught the eyes of Hollywood, which drew upon the incident for its *Wargames*. Eight years later a break-in at Digital Computer that cost, according to the company, $1 million, won him a year in prison, as well as a run of psychological treatment for behavioral difficulties.

In November 1992, he took to his heels and left the real world for good. He had achieved mythic status among hackers, and had escaped without a trace from the scopes of secret services and private investigators. No one had heard from him in a while when, more inaccessible than ever, he managed another assault, this time on an even more important financial institution. No longer content to simply break into company computer systems, stealing, for example, all the credit card numbers from an online provider's client base—twenty thousand alone in San Jose's Netcom—or to deprogram some circuits that annoyed him, he now attacked personal enemies. On one occasion he transferred a hospital's

$30,000 phone bill to one of his relatives. In another prank he routed all the calls destined for a major company's switchboard to a private line, deluging in an interminable flow of calls.

But Mitnick had an Achilles heel, his pride. He decided to take on Tsutomu Shimomura, his old friend who was the only other person in the world who had his level of expertise. Shimomura had not long before been as feared as Mitnick. Now he was selling his services to those who wished to be protected from hackers.

On Christmas day 1994, things began to get ugly. Tsutomu Shimomura realized, just before digging into the holiday ham, that a hacker had found its way into his computer to copy a few marvels. He took the break-in very seriously. A few hours later, representatives of WELL, the main server of Sausalito for Internet access, called one of their clients to report that his account had been exhibiting an unusual level of activity. Considerably surprised, user Bruce Koball looked into the guts of his machine and found that yes, in fact, it had been abnormally active over the past several days. Looking more closely, he saw that one of the computers that his computer had been calling was none other than that of Shimomura. The explanation: to keep his intrusions anonymous, Mitnick had accessed various people's computers via their modems and used them as relays without their owners' knowledge. The access keys and the passwords had been stolen from the providers, and Koball had been chosen by the hacker for both his limited frequency of use and because he was head of a computer information think group called CFP (Computers, Freedom, and Privacy), which organizes a popular conference each year. When the CFP met in Chicago in 1994, the FBI swooped in and arrested someone who looked like him . . . whom they quickly released.

WELL is a monument in cyberspace, and Shimomura, who shares a belief with the Electronic Frontier Foundation that freedom should prevail on the network, found Mitnick's little joke none too funny. So the members of WELL voted and then called the FBI. It was a difficult decision, particularly because WELL had a long history of helping hackers and accommodating the various libertarians of computer information throughout its network. But this time things were different. Mitnick had gone too far, had stepped on too many toes: attacking Shimomura was pushing the limits of what was acceptable. And Shimomura was cut to the quick. The university computer center where he is a senior fellow, SDSC (San Diego Supercomputer Center)—so successful that the NSA had requested its services (which beats all, for a former hacker)—set up a surveillance system of immoderate scope. Everything was dissected in minute detail: the routes Mitnick had traveled for each of his intrusions were pinpointed, and the attacks he had launched against other computers were systematically reconstructed. His tactics were examined with a level of scrutiny equal to his own. But this sort of thing was nothing new: the best counterespionage agents have always been excellent spies. Shimomura narrowed the field by discovering how Mitnick was getting through NetCom and had the FBI watch the company. Despite his many ruses, the source of Mitnick's calls was finally determined. They were all coming from Raleigh, North

Carolina. The city was isolated thanks to the cellular telephone relays he was using.

At 1:30 A.M. on February 15, 1995, the FBI rang Mitnick's doorbell. And Bruce Koball, ardent defender of cryptology, said a few days later: "The irony is while the government spends all its effort chasing after Mitnick, it spends its time trying to suppress the technology that could secure those networks." Koball added: "The Jedi Knight turned to the dark side of the force."[31] Shimomura had won. He could go back to work with the NSA who had contacted him long before, when they had also contacted his friend Dan Farmer, the inventor of SATAN, who didn't take the plunge. One of the world's foremost hackers had collaborated with the world's foremost group of information gatherers, whereas his buddy had created a stunning program, a double-edged sword that protected and attacked.

Mitnick became the antihero, the black sheep. At the end of these exploits, which didn't even bring him much money, he was sent to Wake County prison. Restrictions were imposed upon him unlike those faced by any other convict in the United States: he was not allowed to make a phone call. Having spoken with Shimomura, the prison administration believed that the prisoner could use his talents to erase evidence of his crimes (which may have been giving even him too much technical credit). From jail the only two people he was allowed to call were his mother and his grandmother, and the guards were the ones who actually dialed the phone.

So who is Kevin Mitnick? Is he the sociopath the government would have us believe or "a doof" who never matured beyond adolescence, as Chris Goggans claims? The real answer is perhaps more complicated than either of these. For the postface to a book she wrote about computer hacking in 1991 with John Markoff,[32] Katie Haffner visited Harriet Rosseto, the director of Gateways Beit T'Shuvah (House of Repentance, in Hebrew), the center where Mitnick spent several months in 1989, after he was released from prison on another occasion. This social worker's opinions about Mitnick are interesting, for she believes that he is victim of "an addictive behavior. The closest cousin to Mitnick's affliction," she said, "is gambling. It's not about money or winning: he's addicted to the action."[33] Two books, both published in the wake of Mitnick's arrest, offer fascinating information on this bedlamite. The first, by Tsutomu Shimomura in collaboration with John Markoff,[34] details the tracking of the fugitive by someone who had no love for his prey: the book is written from the point of view of the hunters, by the man who would not give up the hunt until he had caught his man. At the end of the book. Shimomura reveals why he was willing to reveal so much about the nuts and bolts of the hunt: "For me, the real crime is that he violated the original spirit of the hacker ethic. It's not OK to read other people's mail. And to believe that software and computer technologies should be freely shared is not the same as believing that it is OK to steal them."[35]

The other book, often considered to be more comprehensive by the hacking community, was written by Jonathan Littman, who was in touch with Mitnick while he was in hiding.[36] The author believes that "The Condor," Mitnick's cyberspace nickname, was set up to take a fall, in part by someone working for the FBI. The book details Mitnick's mysterious existence and his friendship with Lewis De Payne, his sole link to the larger world. What will become of Kevin Mitnick? On September 26, 1996, the office of the U.S. attorney in San Diego charged the former most wanted hacker with twenty-five counts of felony. It would seem that he is far from being out of judicial hot water.[37]

Intellectual Property . . . for a Steal

No one was safe: in October 1994, hackers managed to break into the systems of the University of Florida and swipe some new software that was being evaluated, notably the beta versions of Microsoft's Windows 95, which the firm's creator and world's richest man, Bill Gates, was expecting to catapult his firm to yet another stratosphere. Today, however, hacker games are no longer as troubling to the economic world. Of course, they still pose a serious menace to the cyberplanet, and hackers still have some beautiful sunsets to look forward to.[38]

The tracking of hackers gave birth to a new breed of police officers: cybercops. They admit that hackers who break into systems for the sake of satisfying their weird sense of fun or even for criminal ends are less important to them than the actual theft of software. To this end, at the beginning of 1995, at the insistence of Microsoft, federal agents in Lexington, Kentucky, broke up the Assassin's Guild on the BBS, which had been harboring hacker servers of hacker clubs such as Pirates with an Attitude and Razor 1911. The results of the seizure were rather impressive: thirteen computers, eleven modems, a satellite antenna, nine gigabytes of data available to the hackers, and forty gigabytes of digitized information, archived since 1992. In the data they seized, the investigators recovered the beta version of Windows 95, available for downloading!

Stealing software is big business. For years the biggest incidence of this kind of theft has involved computer games. Often, users of little Atari and Amiga computers have found this form of acquisition a most convenient and cost-effective means of expanding their favorite leisure activity—adding hundreds of new games to their repertoires. Today, this traffic has far surpassed the humble initiatives of adolescent copy parties. Very sophisticated games, created by firms like Nintendo, have given birth to a juicy trade in copies, calling for elaborate technical means of skirting the protections that safeguard the originals.

Now there's a hacking industry in place that steals and copies the most expensive, advanced programs for desktop publishing, graphic design, architecture, etc. These high-tech burglars first attack servers where beta versions[39] circulate and can be sold, on a parallel network, at the same time as the commercial version and for a fraction of the price. Just as often, hackers acquire a software program (the specialty of "original suppliers"—hackers who steal software and distribute it within the hacker community) and have their crackers break its copy protection. Naturally, this sort of business leads to big losses within the honest part of the industry, a figure that the Business Software Alliance (BSA) fixed at $780 million in France alone, representing the lost profits from the copies supplied by hacker servers and those exchanged between individuals and employees within companies. This figure is one-third of the total losses suffered by the French computer industry because of counterfeiting.

In the United States, the Software Publishers Association (SPA) has been fighting hacking more and more actively in the past few years. In the Internet Universe, where "free-of-charge" was the law of the land, the idea of "lending" software was entirely accepted regardless of its clear illegality. That, however, has changed. In the first trial of its kind, on July 23, 1996, SPA brought Max Butler, an "original supplier" to trial. Butler had uploaded onto the File Transfer Protocol (FTP).[40] So why was Butler tried? It "is a warning to Internet users who believe they can infringe software copyrights without fear of exposure or penalty. Although SPA has no desire to police all Internet users, we will vigorously pursue blatant violations of an ISP's network operations, and of our members' copyrights—the type of conduct alleged in the complaint against Mr. Butler," said Sandra Sellers, SPA vice president of intellectual property education and enforcement. The action, therefore, can be seen as a wake-up call to the Internet, reading: Attention, the good times are over.

If protection of the American market from within is taking on new importance, one should be aware that the strongest attacks on intellectual property rights are being launched from Asia, particularly China and Russia. According to an SPA announcement in February 1996, these two countries are responsible for creating a parallel industry in software manufacture that pays no rights or royalties to the

authors of the work and flies in the face of all existing international copyright legislation. "Virtually a
single illegitimate copy of software could satisfy the
entire country demand. The SPA estimates more
than 90% of business application software used in
Russia and China in 1995 was illegal, with South
Korea and Greece following close behind at an estimated 80%." In these four countries the authorized
software manufacturers are losing up to $700 mil-
lion per year to hacking. Illegal software trafficking
is growing to extraordinary proportions. An example: two hackers were stopped in Hong Kong in May
1996. On them they had twenty CD-ROMs containing software with a resale value of twenty thousand
dollars, as well as all the necessary paraphernalia
for duplicating that software. They had already begun faxing catalogs of the software they were soon
to make available to dozens of companies across the
country.

In May 1996, the tension caused by illegal du-
plication of copyrighted material drove a wedge between China and the United States. The United
States accused China of overlooking the lucrative
activities of its hackers, a figure estimated by the
SPA and the BSA to be $486 million in 1995. Ac-
cording to the U.S. government, in spring of 1996,
thirty-one factories producing tens of millions of CD-
ROMs were still operational, despite a treaty that
had been signed the previous year and which as-
sured the United States that such activities would
be dealt with severely. The United States expressed
its concern over factories located in the Guangxi region of China. One well-known factory in Guilin produced twenty thousand CD-ROMs a day (copies of

programs by Microsoft and others) as well as music CDs. The United States trade representative made some strong demands for retaliatory sanctions rising as high as $3 billion. An agreement was reached on June 17, 1996, when the Chinese finally agreed to close fifteen factories immediately, which put an end to the commercial conflicts and to the threats of sanctions. But it is difficult to see a real end to this problem. Copies of programs are so easy and inexpensive to make that this problem isn't going to go away for good. An end can only come when the codes that protect such software become infallible, and there are a lot of hackers out there making sure that that day remains a very distant tomorrow.

Seen on a planetary scale, hacking programs appears to be an economic catastrophe, figured at $7.5 billion per year by Ken Walsh, president of SPA. This figure is really much higher since Asian markets get software almost free, which was made in China, India, South Korea, and Taiwan.

In June 1992, the German company Cadsoft, tired of watching its software get pillaged, offered a demonstration program for free. But those who installed it in their computers didn't know that it was designed to hunt out software that had been made by the company but had never been properly registered. When it found stolen copies, a message appeared on screen that invited the happy winners to receive a free manual for their program from Cadsoft. But, if they waited by their mailboxes, they soon received a letter from the company's lawyers inviting them to pay damages of DM 6,000. In six months, four hundred people got taken by this technique, including employees of the German counterespionage agency, the BfV (Bundesamt für Verfassungschutz). Other software manufacturers have concentrated their efforts on companies that may use hundreds of copies of the same program and whose fines when caught dwarf the penalties against individual users. How to handle individual infringements remains a problem, as even computer illiterates can easily copy a program; most people do.

Up to now all the intellectual property questions surrounding the rights of authors and of copyrights have arisen as a result of hacker actions. How do you deal with issues of copyright when the Internet allows for the dispersal of huge quantities of information across the globe in a matter of moments? The answer to this question will remain illusive until someone finds a way to restrict the use of all copies of software to the prior payment of a licensing fee. And that isn't likely to happen for some time.

5

Privateers and Buccaneers

Though he's never really broken into any major computer systems, Jean-Bernard Condat is one of the big players on the European hacker Scene. Born in Béziers, France, in 1963, his reputation precedes him in the press and everywhere that hacking, the Internet, the development of networks, and security are discussed. He earns a living by writing books and articles, setting up Web sites, and offering his services to companies that want to bolster the security systems protecting their information.

When Condat calls himself an expert of the first order, his singsong delivery conveys a self-assured boyish charm. It's important to him to reassert his dominance in the hacker world after having worked for many years to penetrate its depths. Though he takes obvious pleasure in his work, he has been of no small help to France's counterespionnage wing, the DST (Center for National Surveillance).[1]

When a Hacker Works for the Police

When he arrived in Paris in April 1989 after completing his degree in musicology and computer science, Condat was already a contender for counter-espionage work. As early as 1983 he was noticed by the DST when he demonstrated a modest, and not even illegal, hacking maneuver on French regional television: he showed he could hook up to the Dialog database in Palo Alto, California, from a phone booth. They took him under their wing and sent him around to hacker conferences. Soaking up the attention, he was good at turning on the charm, even when it came to conning other hackers: "I take what one guy tells me and make another guy think I did it. . . . "

At the end of 1989, Jean-Luc Delacour, Condat's superior at the DST, decided to enter his young colt in his first big race. The mission was outlined to Condat at a bar on rue Nélaton, near the DST's headquarters. In the early eighties there had been talk about a possible connection between the Chaos Computer Club in Hamburg and the KGB, and people wondered whether any French companies had been hit. The DST responded by concocting the CCCF (Chaos Computer Club of France). Condat, as its president, would attract as many young hackers as he could by the beginning of 1990, letting the police know everything about them so they could nab them if they had to.

This was as easily said as done. Condat came to be known as the white wolf for his ability to prowl around unnoticed. Those least suspicious thought the CCCF was a myth; those more paranoid suspected that it was a police front.

Very quickly the CCCF began to attract the attention of the hackers and the media, but, above all, it revealed to the DST those who were throwing copy parties and committing other infractions. At the DST a reliable source confirms: "Condat was like a foot-bridge to the pirate world, but he never did any pirating on our behalf. We used him defensively, to protect our interests, but never as an offensive weapon. But when someone broke into Thomson or Péhiney, for example, he helped us reconstruct their networks. This wasn't very hard for him, really: bragging comes with the territory."

Condat basked in the attention the DST lavished upon him: whenever he called, they'd send out an inspector immediately to monitor an interesting conversation or to update someone's dossier. Whenever he'd leave Paris, he would be accompanied, though not for fear that he'd take off, why would he?—but because the DST didn't want some other police services to get their hands on him.

The DST turned things into a circus. It printed hundreds of T-shirts, which Condat handed out to his flunkies, and thousands of postcards with his face on them. On September 17, 1991, Condat appeared on a TV talk show where I and a few others were invited to talk about spying as it affected the lives of average citizens. The show's host, journalist Daniel Bilalian, told the audience that the police were in the room to guarantee that Condat's demonstrations wouldn't reveal anything too secret. During the show, Condat was fed his lines through an earpiece by his DST boss. The "hacker" explained how he had reserved all the seats on France's high-speed train, the TGV, by getting into the company's computer. The fact that the exploit was actually perpetrated by someone else was immaterial.

One of the people in charge of this affair said recently of Condat that he had been "very able and gutsy, but not particularly discrete." Hackers and those who frequent hacking circles seem to have the same compulsion to tell all to anyone who'll listen. Hacking is dull stuff indeed if you can't brag about what you've done. And if Condat "truly regrets" that he delivered to the DST so many young hackers who had come to him in friendship, he feels certain that many of them were playing the same game: "Everybody talks. But it took its toll on me. People would come to see me, I'd fill out very detailed reports about them for the DST, and two days later the counterespionage guys would go knock on their doors at six in the morning. I shouldn't have done it. Today I should be married with children and have a house and a car, instead of crawling around like a dog. . . ."[2]

Condat says that the games are over. He was arrested in 1991 by police chief Daniel Padoin (now in charge of SEFTI, Service for the Investigation of Information Technology Fraud) and later acquitted for a telephone hacking scheme. Condat remains convinced that he was more a victim of competition over hackers between the various branches of the police than anything else. He had the unpleasant feeling that the DST just dropped him, leaving him to fight off unfounded allegations.

The history of the secret services is filled with people cast off after they outlived their usefulness. But Condat is still an able, highly knowledgeable young man. He is often called on as a consultant and even serves as an expert witness in trials involving hacking. He writes for numerous newspapers and often appears on European television and in Compuserve online forums in France. At the start of 1997 he took the helm of the French office of a German domestic electronic security firm. It remains to be seen if his past will ever really catch up with him.

Hackers' Inferno

In their little game of cat and mouse, hackers rarely land big game. The likelihood of their doing so is limited because as they gain the technical expertise that makes success possible, their notoriety grows to the point where they are found out. As we have seen, some failures have more to do with betrayal, since the integrity of the hacking Scene has been thoroughly compromised by the actions of Condat and others like him. Despite what they like to believe, it is the rare hacker who moves freely through cyberspace. Any and all newsgroups discussing this subject, as well as the hacker servers, are under constant surveillance by the world's police forces.

Often as enthusiastic as they are naive, hackers aren't always aware of the various personal and legal consequences of their actions. In the years since the earliest skirmishes between the wildly imaginative attackers and those they besieged (who often remained aloof to the risks their systems were open to), the judicial system has had the time to catch up. Some of those clever young hackers quickly learned just what their pranks can cost them. In France, the Godfrain Law of 1988 put a legal foot in the door of those wishing to enter major computer systems.[3]

If hackers seem to have had limited success in France after their initial glory days at the beginning of the eighties, it's due to the speed at which their innocent pranks turned sour. The DGSE, and especially the DST, past masters in the art of getting spies to turn coat, have made use of all their tried and true techniques in these areas, as the story of Condat makes clear. None of these bureaus would ever officially admit to this practice, but behind closed doors tongues come untied. If the "victims" aren't particularly eager to talk about it, the reasons are as old as espionage and double agents.

As a group, hackers belong to an exclusive demographic group: young, well-educated students of computer science who scale firewalls in their free time. Their habitats are well known—a few specialized engineering schools and businesses devoted to information security. When their victims get wind of an intrusion (which always happens), it is increasingly rare for a hacker not to get caught eventually. A huge seizure of stolen information or an arrest of someone like Condat usually helps to calm people's nerves temporarily.

A young hacker who gets caught with his hand in the virtual cookie jar often finds he has grabbed something very hard to let go of. Sometimes the police allow the judicial system to run its course, and the hacker finds himself or herself before a judge, with all the inconveniences that implies: tribunals have no sympathy for hackers. Sometimes, like spies caught *in flagrante delicto*, the hackers are asked if they would like to put an end to their selfish pursuits and collaborate with the police. Ratting on a few friends isn't good enough. Nothing short of signing on with the secret services themselves will do. Few hackers have been able to refuse these "invitations" over the past several years, particularly those caught around their twenty-first birthdays, the age when French boys do their year of military service.

When a hacker turns coat, working for the police can turn a nightmare into a dream come true. For no matter how adept a hacker may be at intercepting communications on their way to computers (passwords, secret codes, etc.), they are no match for the police when it comes to information that is more vulnerable to traditional investigation techniques: passwords that are variations on users' personal information—birthdays, names of pets, a phrase written on a piece of paper next to a monitor. And the specific information-gathering expertise of the investigator, when coupled with the hackers' facility with code-breaking software, can make for a very fruitful collaboration.

For hackers, this is business, not fun and games. They steal into bank computers to observe the accounts of suspects, try to cause crashes, or even to withdraw funds. They enter secret doors in personal computers (at least in those with modems). And even if they don't, not all is lost. Hackers have found ways of supplying users whose computers they wish to access with modems. Many unsuspecting victims have received free modems in the mail and have, presumably without a second thought, connected them up and started using them.

Hackers can then use "sniffing" programs that intercept the user's login (access code) and call back at a time when the risks of encountering the authorized user are low. Sometimes, this isn't so easy. Techniques exist that help camouflage a computer's identification codes, including electronic remailers available on the networks, which make it possible to hide the address of a message one sends by shuttling it through a series of successive nodes; anonymous servers such as these have been in place since 1994 (thanks to Johann Helsingius in Finland[4]), and protect the identities of those who hook up to them. In fact, the anonymous Finnish server wouldn't have prevailed forever. On August 30, 1996, Helsingius announced that he was ending his service, an announcement confirmed by the Finnish government, citing a complaint by the Church of Scientology and asserting that Helsingius's practices were against Finnish law.[5] Helsingius sent an explanation of his decision over the Internet: "I will close down the remailer for the time being because the legal issues governing the whole Internet in Finland are yet undefined. The legal protection of the users needs to be clarified. At the moment the privacy of Internet messages is judicially unclear. . . . These remailers have made it possible for people to discuss very sensitive matters, such as domestic violence, school bullying or human rights issues anonymously and confidentially on the Internet. To them the closing of the remailer is a serious problem." A forceful critique of Helsingius that appeared in England's *Observer* a few days before the closing had little to do with the decision. The article, drawing heavily on unsubstantiated claims, accused Helsingius of having allowed the transmission of child pornography over his server. The facts, to which even the Finnish police were later to admit, were that Helsingius himself had taken precautions in 1995 to make the transmission of child pornography technically impossible.[6] Today, no one can guarantee that the source of an attack won't be discovered. Even the secret services have come to learn this. As a result, it should come as no surprise that most countries' foreign embassies keep their computer systems off networks, any networks. It's just too risky.

Tempest Rains on Aldrich Ames

Aldrich Ames, whose arrest I described earlier, is a bastard straight out of a spy novel. Having spent years working for the CIA in charge of managing Soviet spies that American (and some British) agents had rooted out, he managed to betray his employer with an astounding regularity and a boundless enthusiasm. When he was found out in 1993, the FBI wanted to know all that Ames was capable of before nabbing him. When the team of super investigator Leslie G. Wiser was told to build up a case file against him, they immediately sought to break into Ames's home personal computer. Unfortunately (at least for the FBI), the CIA employee wasn't yet connected to the Internet (his computer didn't even have a modem); he was still typing out his messages to his KGB bosses and leaving them at Washington dropoffs. This just goes to show that the best protection against such tactics still remains not hooking up to a network, although this is becoming practically unrealisic these days with the popularity of the Internet. Since his computer wasn't connected to anything, the FBI's investigators decided to make use of a little-known technique that allowed for the interception by radio receivers of electromagnetic impulses emitted by Ames's computer.

Those who use PCs at home or in the office and who want to keep their information to themselves should know that their computers are, for all intents and purposes, radio transmitters. The keyboard, the CPU, the connection cables, the monitor, and the printer all constitute sources of electromagnetic radiation. Specialists call these emissions "compromising parasite signals" or "red signals," and somewhat sophisticated radio receivers like the Dynamic Science A-110b (1 kHz–1 GHz) are able to pick them up easily. These electromagnetic waves have been known and studied on a grand scale since the early sixties. At the prompting and technical direction of the NSA, Tempest has has become the standard in anti-intrusion efforts. It is so secret that the engineers who came up with the system and the name won't even spell out the acronym they gave it. There are lots of ideas for what it stands for, but the two most plausible seem to be Total Electronic and Mechanical Protection against Emissions of Spurious Transmissions, or Terminal Electromagnetic Pulse Environment Safeguard Technique.

Aldrich Ames nearly became one of the first official victims of this technique. Sometimes these red signals are believed to travel hundreds of yards; in Ames's case, the FBI ran tests finding that the signals went no farther than 82 yards from the $500,000 house he shared with his wife Rosario.[7] The house, for which they had paid cash (without setting off alarms at the CIA), is in an isolated residential Washington, DC, neighborhood; a professional agent like Ames would have immediately noticed a surveillance van had it been parked nearby. So the FBI thought it would be better if Ames were sent away for a few days.

Searches are the meat and potatoes of the spying biz, and they've been refined to an art form. Using elaborate techniques that conform to their meticulous reconnaissance of a site, agents can infiltrate and leave no trace of their presence, making detection of the break-in nearly impossible. In addition to the installation of dozens of microphones in Ames's luxury home, the visit allowed agents to make a copy of Ames's hard drive. A specialist rummaged through his drive and found communications to the Russians that Ames thought he had lost.[8]

One wonders, in light of the recent rash of arrests, how many moles remain in the American information-gathering sphere. With greed as the prime motivation for such criminal activities, the prospects of further discoveries are regrettably good. Take the example of Harold J. Nicholson, arrested in November 1996. Nicholson was the CIA's Bucharest bureau chief in the early eighties before moving to the Kuala Lumpur office. In 1994 he began spying for the Russians. As a chief in charge of new CIA recruits at Camp Peary, not far from Williamsburg, Virginia, Nicholson gave the names of all his students to his Russian liasons, who rewarded him handsomely for his simple service. Furthermore, using his high security clearance, Nicholson accessed classified documents on the CIA's computer and made them available to the Russians. On March 3, 1997, he pled guilty before the Alexandria, Virginia, federal court. His plea saved him from serving a life sentence, though not by much. Three days later a former FBI agent, Earl Pitts, also pled guilty to spying for the Russians. Though the information to which he had access was of a much less sensitive nature, Pitts had been spying for the Russians since 1984.

Though software exists that can alert users to the sort of break-ins that have caught many spies (as well as other software that can block a would-be copier's invasive efforts), Aldrich Ames was thoroughly unprotected. One expert has confirmed that at the time they were doing this, the FBI could have easily installed a real radio transmitter within the computer (no doubt connected to the keyboard circuit) that would have allowed the agents to pick up a very clean signal from a comfortable distance.

Ames was put out to pasture a few months later, and in April 1994, after he admitted his guilt, he made a deal with the authorities that avoided a public trial and saved his wife from prosecution. The charges against him concerned his espionage work for the USSR and tax evasion for not reporting the $4.6 million he was paid by the KGB. Everything purchased with the money was seized, except for property he had bought in Colombia where his wife Rosario was from. (Ames and Rosario had met in Mexico, where she worked at the Colombian embassy; he had been sent there by the CIA.) He was condemned to spend the rest of his life in prison, without chance of parole.

Tempest French Style

In the late eighties, at the French Defense Ministry in Paris, some of the high-ups received unexpected visits. Army technicians, specialists in network security, took great pleasure waltzing into the offices of various government bigwigs and suggesting that they take a peek inside a truck parked on the street below. There they saw the very screens that, in their offices above, their secretaries were working on, intercepted and reproduced on remote PC screens where they, or anyone, could witness the secretaries' keystrokes appearing from out of thin air. CELAR (The Electronic Arms Center),[9] which recently demonstrated these techniques to a few journalists, of whom I was one,[10] started a vast movement aimed at awakening military computer users to the indiscretions to which their machines were vulnerable.

No law prohibits the interception of computer radio waves, nor are most users, whether private, public, or industrial, even mildly aware of the risks to their privacy, given the ease with which secret services can read the computer information of individual users, as if it were a book left open on a tabletop.

Under certain conditions the use of laptop computers can limit access to information, since they emit less radiation than coventional desktop models. Sometimes, the Orwellian observers who specialize in these interceptions find themselves at a loss to isolate the emissions of a single computer in a room of one hundred: it is nearly impossible to discriminate between them.

Much in the way that certain levels of cryptology are reserved only for the government so as to allow the secret services to flip through the files of average citizens, Tempest, too, has not been available to the public or even to businesses who have not received special permission. Naturally, this protects the authorities most who wish to safeguard their machines, but it also ensures that they can go on intercepting the emissions of others.

The United States got Tempest up and running in 1974. A PC protected by the system is a cross between a desk and a bunker. The idea is to change any part of the system that broadcasts its presence into a miniature Faraday cage,[11] which is to say into an enclosure that prevents radio waves from escaping. Mainframe computers protected by Tempest look like tanks: the shielded cables are enormous, the special secured connectors are elephantine. Only the screens of the computers remain apparently unchanged, protected by a thin metallic latticework that is nearly invisible. In the United States, more than fifty companies manufacture components of Tempest hardware,[12] however, manufacturing these parts to the high standards demanded by Tempest's creators can double the cost of equipment.

But for the most sensitive diplomatic installations, cost is no object. Entire rooms are designed on the Faraday cage principle and made emissions-tight, Tempest computers installed within. One can't be too careful: even the slightest opening in the "cage" can allow radio waves to fly away like a flock of sparrows. One user of all this hardware tells the story of a night watchman charged with guarding one such Faraday cage. In a routine scan of emissions, technicians found that despite all the safeguarding and special measures, radio waves were still seeping out. It took the technicians a few minutes, but they soon figured out the problem: bored silly, the night watchman had drilled a hole in the wall so that he could run a TV antenna cable into the room since his antenna wouldn't pick up any signals within the Faraday cage (by design!). The hole was quickly plugged and the Faraday cage was once again secure.

The Tempest standard served as the basis for the first cybernovel, *Terminal Compromise*, available only on the Internet.[13] Written by Winn Schwartau, one of the top computer security experts in the United States, the novel explores a provocative scenario: Japanese revenge against the United States for their victory in World War II, a revenge through intrusions into U.S. computer systems. The new guru of economic intelligence, Robert D. Steele, whose company Open Source Solutions is gobbling up important sectors of the world economy, believes that ignorance of the importance of Tempest is causing huge losses: "Most U.S. companies do not have a full appreciation of how easily others can penetrate their organizations, and most do not engage in significant industrial espionage. For instance, most U.S. companies have absolutely no computer security and no measures to protect their computers from external penetration. They are completely unaware of the ease with which computer screens and computer emissions can be captured from a van parked outside their building. There is a general sense among U.S. firms that industial espionage is 'not worth it.'"[14]

An Attack on British Telecom

The secret services are not safe from hacker attacks. One of the most extraordinary assaults in recent memory occurred in Great Britain in 1994, when a hacker who made his way into the computers of British Telecom (Britain's main phone company) was able to uncover its most secret material: lists of home phone numbers of all members of government, including then prime minister John Major, as well as the numbers of all the heads of Britain's secret services: MI6 (foreign service), MI5 (domestic service), and GCHQ (Government Communications Headquarters), the branch responsible for security breaks.

The story, which caused a huge uproar, was broken in the *Independent* by journalist Steve Fleming, who had received the ultraconfidential information from the hacker via the Internet and an anonymous server. The hacker explained that he had gotten himself hired as a temp at British Telecom after discovering that its big central computer had a few "interesting" vulnerabilities. He had even found the secret codes of company functionaries flickering on the screens of their computers, giving free access to the list of the most unlisted numbers in Britain: they had left them there so that the temps filling in while they were on vacation would have no trouble accessing the ultraprotected central system. Preventing such catastrophically foolish cases of human error that fully undermine all the high-tech firewalls and hacker-fighting software is apparently a greater challenge than one might have thought.

6

The Golden Age of Cybercops

Most domains depend heavily on computers: the military, big business, education, and armed forces. Though society could function without them, few would deny the powerful role they now play in our daily lives, from the barcode readers in supermarkets to high-speed tollbooths, from word processing to air traffic control. Companies are establishing networks of their own through which their employees may communicate, and more and more nomads are working out of the office, hooking up cellularly to colleagues they come to know as disembodied voices and bundles of bits.

The High-Stakes World of Information Security

The dependability and integrity of these systems are essential. A huge computer error could paralyze a company or a country. Journalists, for instance, are well aware that the most minor of computer disasters can send editorial offices into pandemonium. And hacking isn't their only worry. Researchers have made great progress in dealing with hackers and are now fighting on other fronts. Disasters can be brought on by many means other than intrusion: fires, software failures, and a host of others. CERT (the Computer Emergency Response Team) at Carnegie-Mellon University is still the model for virtual SWAT teams and has been imitated throughout Europe. NIST (the National Institute of Standards and Technology) has launched FIRST (Form of Incident Response and Security Team) out of its National Computer Systems Laboratory. FIRST is a network of experts across the country who react immediately via the Internet to various emergency situations. Computer crimes originating from inside companies whose dishonest operators can cause major debacles (often financial) have become the subject of exhaustive study. [1]

In Europe the French have their own comprehensive computer security club called CLUSIF,[2] a branch of APSAD (a plenary assembly of insurance companies).[3] In an assessment of the years 1986 through 1990, CLUSIF reported that the biggest computer disasters involved embezzlement and virtual sabotage, and that the internal hackers or "mutineers" who engineered them were no less creative than their hacker counterparts. One difference, however, was the size of the game the mutineers landed. Simple, clever techniques have instantly netted hundreds of thousands of dollars for wrongdoers, and those taking full advantage of the computerization of the world banking system have really raked it in. One mutineer rigged a phony transfer of $16 million at a bank in Zurich, Switzerland, at the same time that he sent a phony order for that dollar amount for diamonds from Moscow, all through the same bank. The Swiss bank paid for the diamonds and sent them to their client, but the money from America that was supposedly the basis for the whole deal never arrived. With a simple dummy entry for currency exchange rates, someone at another bank earned an instant $1.5 million.

Hackers do find their way into the CLUSIF report, too, even if the names of the companies attacked do not. The German Chaos Computer Club attacked the telephone switchboard of a savings bank in order to feed through thirteen thousand calls that cost the bank eighty thousand dollars. During the same period, another bank spent ten times that much to rid its system of a simple virus. However, the world record for this sort of sabotage goes to the evil few who destroyed an unnamed bank's security systems and all record of its accounts. This bit of violence cost the bank $20 million.

In some circumstances, investigators aren't able to find the perpetrators of the misdeeds. But computer professionals, along with the secret services and the new breed of cybercop, are always looking for better ways to beef up any system's security (which a new generation of hackers, before going to work for the Feds, will try to bypass). In the interim, CLUSIF is trying to make companies aware that how willing and able they are to protect their computer information can be a gauge of their likelihood to survive. According to Jean-Marc Alloüet, the secretary-general of CLUSIF: "The value of the contents of a computer system, even a home computer system, is rarely less than ten times the worth of the machine itself." This will no doubt come as a surprise to most users.

Even Paranoids Have Enemies

Despite the apparent freedoms that the Internet offers and that its boosters like to assert, the secret services have clearly been transforming these tools of freedom into new means of social surveillance. And as military use of the Internet as a weapon of war has proliferated, its practical freedoms seem increasingly illusory. The line grows fainter between the undeniable advantages of instant communications and the concomitant disadvantages of increased governmental intrusions into citizens' private lives. As early as 1977, the U.S. Privacy Protection Study Commission noted: "The real danger is the gradual erosion of individual liberties through the automation, integration, and interconnection of many small, separate record-keeping systems, each of which alone may seem innocuous, even benevolent, and wholly justifiable."[4] Despite the attempts of lawmakers to block the inevitable, clearly the visionaries have carried the day.[5]

George Orwell had, of course, anticipated all of this back in 1948 when he wrote *1984*. Big Brother, Orwell's idea of an omnipresent governmental observer peering into the lives of his fictional citizens, is now living among us. It would be as shortsighted to ignore his presence as it would be to conclude that there is nothing we can do to protect against his electronic eye watching public and private sectors.

John O'Leary of the Computer Security Institute (CSI) admits that "the civil libbers are yelling and screaming over the privacy issue. But it isn't realistic."[6] Claude-Marie Vadrot and Louisette Gouverne, co-authors of a book on the subject of modern means of social control, which has attracted considerable attention in France, believe that society has come up against a sort of "computing totalitarianism" and that "a group of high-level programmers in government and in the private sector is in the process of waging a successful technological coup d'état that manufacturers eyeing the security and verification market are doing everything to assist."[7] This may be going too far.

However, the self-styled realists who argue that secret services can't possibly hope to monitor hundreds of simultaneous telephone calls, let alone scan a network as vast as the Internet, are overlooking the huge strides being made in artificial intelligence and analysis tools such as plaintext. Since 1994, IBM has had a system available to PC owners that allows instantaneous transcription of dictation into a written text, a virtual stenographer. Even the most immune to knee-jerk paranoia can see how such a tool, long in the hands of the secret services, could be used for the automatic transcription of telephone communications into digital text. As we'll see in the following chapter, analysis "engines" like Taiga and Topic can generate instant summaries of documents that highlight key words and concepts.

Of course, most of the world's police agencies are not quite this sophisticated, at least not yet. Such advanced means are only at the disposal of the NSA, Britain's GCHQ, France's DGSE, Germany's BND, and Russia's SVR. Most of their activities are still so secret that it is nearly impossible to pin down the current levels of their expertise, which is entirely dependent on the how much number-crunching power they have in their arsenals.

Can You Say "Security Crazy"?

Anyone who has perused his or her monthly statement from the phone company knows how much our privacy is threatened. What does the statement tell us? The numbers we called, the day we called them, and the amount of time we were connected. From this information, a stranger would get a good picture of our acquaintances. As yet, there's no way of stopping this sort of information from being compiled, and there is little to prevent it from being used by those curious about the company we keep.

In businesses, the persons in charge of a company's telecommunications can tell when any employee makes a call and who has been called, and then use modern methods (PABX, Private Automatic Branch Exchange) of statistical analysis to break down the calls. They can determine how often calls were placed to a given country and whether they were business related. There is nothing to stop managers from gathering this sort of information.

Does your company give you free Internet access? It's a mixed blessing: your administrator knows exactly what servers are being called. If they're related to the company's needs, fine; but if the employee is hooking up to interactive games or is downloading naughty photographs, nothing prevents the boss from finding out. Normally, those in charge have bigger fish to fry than employee mischief. But in the event of a dispute, it shouldn't come as a surprise if this sort of information suddenly appeared. If such corporate surveillance seems far-fetched, guess again. There are numerous examples of companies that observe their computers around the clock, not simply to see when people clock in and out, but to observe what their workers are doing. Programmers have given managers the ability to receive a direct feed from any employee's workstation and to watch what that employee is seeing on his or her screen.

No one is safe from intrusions like this, not even journalists. In Paris it's not unusual for some journalists to find their computer screens suddenly seize up for a few minutes. No reason to panic: it's just the editors of the paper verifying, via a "mirror" of the journalist's screen, that work is moving along. A program called Timbuktu, made by Farallon, is excellent for such applications and allows a supervisor to take remote control of a computer equipped with the same program. As long as all the telephones and modems are properly set up, a supervisor in New York can observe the work in progress of an employee in Los Angeles, making Timbuktu the perfect intracompany surveillance tool. Other programs on the market such as Close-Up/LAN by Norton Lambert, Peak & Spy by Dynamic, LANlord by Microcom, and NetMinder by Neon software are all packaged as means of "improving organization" and "increasing productivity," but actually " . . . they turn employees' cubicles into covert listening stations. Other software applications count the number of keystrokes per minute, the employee's error rate, the time it takes to complete each task, and the time a person spends away from the computer. Not surprisingly, the Orwellian potential of such technology has privacy advocates and working stiffs a bit paranoid."[8]

Overseeing productivity in the workplace isn't the end of it. Via other systems, employee movements can be tracked so that the employer knows exactly where they are at any moment. Using modern policing tools, employers can make sure that only certified employees are entering the workplace and that friends, family members, or evildoers aren't sneaking in too. Magnetic entry ID cards aren't enough, nor is fingerprint identification sufficient. Biomechanics has become much more sophisticated: comparisons of our auricles, retinas, and voices to the "originals" stored on the security computer allow instant perfect verification of identity. If that isn't creepy enough, it gets worse. . . .

Zero Inventory and Tracking

One of the best examples of how the logic of networking has changed business involves traffic flow: trains, long- and short-haul truckers, and public service vehicles have all been affected. Overnight shipping companies such as Federal Express, United Parcel Service, and DHL have profoundly altered their way of doing business due to new technology. Most drivers carry cellular telephones, and some of their trucks are equipped with satellite antennas that can tell their bosses exactly where they are, even if they'd rather not. Military carriers use similar satellite technology, their trucks often outfitted with small antennas which relay their positions via satellite back to earth.

All over the world, rapid advancements are being made, and the old concept of warehousing is being replaced by zero inventory and tracking. Both of these systems ensure that companies never stock items they don't need—saving them the huge expense of stockpiling hundreds, perhaps thousands of as yet unnecessary items—and instead receive them on an as-needed basis. Computerized tracking allows items to be requested instantly via computer, which then arrive by one of the overnight delivery services (which can track each of their packages from pickup to delivery). Talk about instant gratification!

Tracking vehicle movements via radiolocation or radar has long been done by the military, using systems such as DECCA or Loran C. A new system, GPS Navstar, is a network of twenty-four geostationary satellites launched by the Pentagon that can track the movements of individual soldiers to within a few feet of their actual position (viewers of the film *Patriot Games* got to see a mock-up of this system in action). Rather than requiring an elaborate complex of machines and technicians to process this information, GPS data can be received on portable devices barely larger than pocket calculators. They can even be installed in the guidance systems of missiles. Less precise versions of the same technology (allowing accuracy of 100 to 1000 feet) are sold for a few hundred dollars to yachtsmen, hikers, and owners of shipping companies. The companies that market these commercially available tracking systems offer a dazzling array of optional equipment, including integrated portable computers, optical code readers, and GPS receivers, all of it connected in real time to company headquarters.

Trucking has had to become high-tech to keep pace with new methods of warehousing, such as zero inventory. In a remarkable article in *Wired*, readers learned about the new life of Walt Maguire, a truck driver whose employer, Schneider National, installed a computer in his cab.[9] Maguire hated the computer the moment he saw it, and as he lived with it his hatred only increased. His new companion was hooked up via satellite to the OmniTRACS network. OmniTRACS relays information, such as speed, revolutions per minute, gas mileage, and location to an accuracy of 100 feet, back to Schneider and other trucking companies. This is a nightmare for truckers like Maguire, who chose trucking for the freedom of the open road.

Computers and Liberty

Students of human social behavior would have a field day comparing the approaches of various countries to the issue of "confidential information." In the United States, it's almost impossible to access information about the fiscal health of a privately held company, whereas in France such information is available on many databases. On the other hand, information about driving records, personal medical history, and credit ratings are all easily accessible in the United States, whereas in France this personal information is carefully guarded by medical and governmental oversight groups. The law prevents them from releasing the information to anyone. Of course, if the right people have the will, there's always a way.

To help benefit from whatever knowledge is available on potential suspects, European police services have been making inroads toward partnership with one another. Despite disappointments and difficulties in putting a practical system into play (named C-SIS for Schengen Information System),[10] persistence has won out, and the European police bureaus now have shared access to a database of pan-European information. However, not everyone is waving flags and cheering over this sort of success.

Two specialists complain: "We're caught in a spider's web, a miniature Big Brother built out of all the computerized information being compiled about our movements. Although the impetus for all this information-gathering isn't intentionally totalitarian, history makes clear that democratic societies, aware that the future is unknown, shouldn't allow for the gathering of sensitive personal information that could be used against the citizenry in a time of crisis."[11] Seen from this angle, each of CNIL's (a national commission on computers and liberty)[12] reports details a host of mini judicial battles waged against the organization by the supporters of free access to files. One recent report exposed the recently launched MUGA-Terrorism file (Unified Management of Terrorist Archives) set up by the police of southwest France. The file earmarks particular potential terrorist activities in this heavily Basque region.[13]

An Eye on Islam

Activist groups using the Internet as a means of communication are often under close observation by secret services, so a lot is being made of the spread of Islamic fundamentalism across cyberspace. The GIA (Armed Islamic Group),[14] responsible for various bloody incidents in Algeria, has been blowing its horn on the Internet via San Diego's AIG (American Islamic Group). In the United States, the Internet is proving to be an excellent means of recruiting new adherents, particularly from universities, into the Islamic fold. During the summer of 1994, a member of New York's Algerian community reported that "at Brooklyn's Polytechnic Institute, fifteen out of twenty North African professors were ardent Islamic Front sympathizers."

The Internet's appeal to militants is understandable: instant global intercommunication. Often, legitimate groups such as the AANA (Algerian American National Association) or the IANA (Islamic Assembly of North America) are unwittingly used as fronts by militants who use their mailing lists to disperse their views.

In universities across the United States, Moslem students have created webs devoted to the discussion of Islam. Though these webs are often closely monitored by administrators, university officials have wisely made no efforts to intrude. At Ohio State University, Islamic students post their newsletter "MSA News" (often containing twenty new articles a day) on all Islamic Internet centers, as well as making available a "World Islam Resource Guide" that gives the addresses of over two hundred sources of further information (both virtual and actual) in twenty-nine countries. Using false identities, secret services have subscribed to all of these letters to get the inside scoop on militant activities and ideas. But it's not always easy to find your way back along the Internet to the source of information. Experts know perfectly well how to hide or even fake their electronic addresses. To succeed at such tricky maneuvers, one must be operating on a UNIX network, an operating system found on very high power computers. The police also scrupulously study the discussion groups on the USENET network to spot conversations on the subject or to pick out potenial new "clients." During the research for this book, I came upon information that I could not confirm that Islamic militants are connected to the Internet from within the heart of the French Defense Ministry.

Militias and Neo-Nazis

If the cybercops seem to be paying close attention to Moslems on the Internet, neo-Nazis don't seem to be worrying them. Nonetheless, these hate-mongers are very active and are being hounded by "digital commandos" who cruise the Net trying to spot advocates of anti-Semitism and other offensive points of view. There are numerous newsgroups like "alt.revisionism," where the chat runs along all too familiar lines. However, one finds similar sentiments being expressed in less likely places—newsgroups on the First and Second World Wars, as well as on twentieth-century history. Groups discussing fetishism may address the symbolism of Nazi uniforms, while others discussing "pure" ideologies will quickly devolve into patter about sorcery and Satan worship.

The most frequent response to these occasional spasms of hate is general intolerance, leading members of the cybercommunity to take things into their own hands. One means of stymieing hate speech online has been to send continuous barrages of messages through to a newsgroup, preventing its members from getting a word in. Also, by pinpointing the server where the newsgroup originates, hackers can usually retaliate with basic hacker strategies.

In Los Angeles, the Simon Wiesenthal Center, under the direction of Rabbi Abraham Cooper, has long been ferreting out Nazis: lately, they have been making extensive use of the Net to do so. Rick Eaton, a researcher there who spends his day in front of various keyboards and screens, relates, not without some dread, that "extremist groups have learned to use the Net, allowing them access to a much greater part of the world. Most Internet users aren't interested in their propaganda, but the more you diversify, the greater your chances are of attracting new clients."[15] In fact, the presence of neo-Nazi and other extremists on the Internet is a real problem. In France, by law no server can disseminate racist propaganda or denials of the holocaust as historical fact. But this law doesn't hold for most other western democracies, particularly the United States, where freedom of expression is the law of the land. So in this interconnected world of ours, nothing could be easier than for a French Websurfer to connect to a U.S. or Scandinavian Nazi server. Thus, despite local efforts, the Internet defies all legislative restriction by its very form. Robert Faurisson, a former French University professor, who was run off his post due to legal troubles stemming from his other role as leader of the negationists (those who deny the existence of the Holocaust) wrote in 1996: "Thanks chiefly to the Internet, the winds of change are blowing in the direction of revisionist history. For the first time in twenty years, I am not in court."[16] Dozens of Nazi sites bloom around the world and over the Internet, taking advantage of the phenomenal opportunities that the network of networks allows all who wish to spread seeds of good and evil. What to do? In 1996 the UEJF (French Jewish Students United)[17] lodged a formal complaint against nine Parisian access providers—those companies through which individuals and companies wishing to connect to the Internet receive service. Though the complaint had little legal merit (as providers themselves would be hard pressed to search the sum total of sites and chat rooms available with the world of individual possibilities), the underlying frustration it signaled marked the complaint as an important sign of protest and social unrest. In October 1996, the French Association of Internet Professionals (AFPI)[18] circulated a long statement specifying those rights and duties it felt responsible to uphold, fundamentally a desire "to inform users of the network's customs and laws" and to see that those providers associated with AFPI strive to maintain a consistent level of Internet decency.

While the world network remains unfazed by local attempts at governmental limitations to access, free speech on the Net often comes with footnotes. A German militant Nazi, Ernest Zundel, creator of "Zundelsite," benefited from the support of several groups within the Internet community: they helped establish links from their sites to his, but not without criticizing him on their welcome pages. On February 2, 1997, at the largest gathering of the French Jewish community, Judeoscope, debate raged over the proper response to the growing tide of negationists, anti-Semites, and other racists. And while no permanent answers to these perennial plagues have been found, the Internet is proving to be the latest incarnation of an evolving shelter for both the best and worst of human impulses.

7

Information Wars

The history of warfare is, among other things, the history of technology. Every era has its weapon of mass destruction—massive Napoleonic armies, the rifle, the machine gun, the battleships of the nineteenth century, tanks and planes at the beginning of the twentieth, and nuclear weapons at the century's center. As we approach the end of a century that has been one long list of technological leaps forward, computers are radically impacting the balance of military power and revolutionizing how we conceive of armed conflict. As always, information about one's adversaries ("They plan to attack at dawn," or "Hey: don't bring that wooden horse in here") helps win wars. Systems now exist that can integrate information gathered from satellites as well as spies, giving commanders a tactical advantage. What's more, the architects of modern warfare depend on them.[1]

The major international powers watch everything: satellite images, radar, computer activity in and out of a country, and military telephone and computer communications. All this information serves to inform their commanders and soldiers, but perhaps more surprisingly it is also used to orient public opinion in support of particular military goals.

But the information war has its limitations. It is most effective against adversaries of similar technological expertise, particularly those with democratic governments whose people remember wars fought on their own soil. But information war can also turn the tide against the most technologically proficient power. The American initiative in Somalia in 1992 and 1993 ended with one symbolic image: the naked body of a helicopter pilot dragged behind a rebel militia vehicle through streets filled with cheering onlookers. The image was sent instantly across CNN and all the networks, and American public opinion quickly coalesced against all that the image implied. Information war, much in the manner of old fashioned propaganda, can still be waged outside of cyberspace. A single television image, beamed via satellite, had a profound impact on all those who watched.

Network versus Kalachnikov

Nonetheless, in its own way, cyberspace has become a battlefield. Since the launching of Operation Desert Shield in Iraq in August 1991, there have been many major technological advances. A new network called DSNET 2 (Desert Shield Net) was put into place that safeguarded ultrasensitive digital information from the battlefield on up. But not all the innovations pioneered in that era were successfully implemented during the conflict. An astounding example of reliance on old-fashioned methods of communication involved antimissile alert satellites monitoring Iraqi Scud missiles. Within fractions of a second, this information was relayed not to Saudi Arabia but to a base in Colorado Springs, Colorado, that would call in coordinates by telephone to the Patriot missile batteries protecting Jerusalem and Tel Aviv, which in turn would have a few seconds to launch a counterstrike before the Scuds would hit. Such roundabout systems made a new communications network a top priority.

The Pentagon, which uses the Automatic Digital Network (Autodin) for its communications, supplemented it with an Automated Message Handling System (AMHS) specially designed to allow military information analysts to "have a real-time picture of military and political trends around the world,"[2] all of which is integrated into the Defense Data Network (DDN). The Pentagon also decided to add the Defense Message System–Government Open Systems Interconnection Profile network (DMS-GOSSIP), set up by the Loral company in the summer of 1995. But on this terrain, military and civil engineers have been making advances at blinding speeds, putting systems in place no one had dreamed of before the Gulf War: "Many of the most critical information systems used to distribute target and battle information during Desert Storm did not exist on the day that Iraq invaded Kuwait. Instead, they were improvised, on the spot, by technicians who, upon discovering that communications and computer equipment would be late in arriving and lacked range, capacity and connectivity to meet operational needs, contrived networks by unorthodox and unauthorized use of agglomerations of military and civilian informationware."[3]

This problem has been dealt with by integrating networks into the heart of the intelligence business: networks are now a linchpin in the overall arsenal. As the Pentagon's assistant director for strategic planning makes clear, there's no longer any question of doing without: "On today's electronic frontier, information with a wide range of utility and relevance is readily accessible by nations, transnational groups, and individuals. The seamless correlation of opensource information with classified intelligence sources is absolutely necessary to maintaining our advantage. [. . .] Finally, our ability to suppress, infiltrate, corrupt or destroy an adversary's information systems will obviously improve the information differential. Both lethal means and traditional electronic warfare can deny an enemy access to its own information. America's commercial dominance in the realm of information technology has empowered our armed forces with the capability to conduct information-based warfare. To date, this capability has augmented the traditional forms of warfare. However, as the information age matures, a truly revolutionary form of warfare will emerge. Information warfare will be fought in a different environment, with adversaries grappling in cyberspace. As every potential adversary achieves access to multiple information systems, warfare will be conducted virtually at the speed of light over global distances. Domination of cyberspace may render the need to employ conventional forces and and firepower less likely."[4]

Clearly, the United States has been making huge advances in its computer armamentation, moving well beyond its closest rivals in Europe and elsewhere, to the extent that in August 1995 they opened an officer training school specializing in the study of information war, conjuring the notion of some future digital battlefield in which all deaths will be virtual, as if part of some giant video game.

The lead had been taken by the U.S. Air Force, which in one fell swoop in 1993 bought 300,000 PCs and opened an Information Warfare Center. General Kenneth Minihan, then head of intelligence for the Air Intelligence Agency, made his feelings clear about what he called "information dominance": This opinion takes on added weight with the knowledge that General Minihan led one of the most brilliant careers in espionage in all the intelligence community. After heading the Defense Intelligence Agency (DIA) from September 1995, he took charge of the NSA in February 1996. He has his own theories about information war: "Information dominance is not 'my pile of information is bigger than yours' in some sort of linear sense. It is not just a way to reduce the fog of war on our side or thicken it on the enemy's side. It is not analysis of yesterday's events, although proper application of historical analysis is important to gaining information dominance. It is something that is battled for, like air superiority. It is a way of increasing our capabilities by using that information to make right decisions, and apply them faster than the enemy can. It is a way to alter the enemy's entire perception of reality. It is a method of using all information at our disposal to predict (and affect) what happens tomorrow, before the enemy even jumps out of bed and thinks about what to do today. Most of all, information dominance is a mind set. It is the attitude needed to make ourselves a powerful weapon on the battlefields of the 21st century."[5]

This technological imperative is at the heart of new U.S. Army doctrine, Force XXI. This idea of information dominance is now at the heart of U.S. Army strategic concepts. In a fat and fascinating doctrinal document titled *Field Manual 100-6* (FM 100-6), priorities are made perfectly clear: "The Army is embracing a new era characterized by the accelerating growth of information, information sources, and information dissemination capabilities supported by information technology. This new era, the so-called Information Age, offers unique opportunities as well as some formidable challenges. New technology will enhance the Army's ability to achieve situational dominance on land, where the decisive element of victory for our nation has always been critical. At the same time, it will enable adversaries to employ many of these same capabilities. This new technology also allows the Army to transform itself."[6]

The United States armed forces have invested heavily in computerized combat simulation technology called SIMNET, which allows for training through virtual engagement. As a result, when eighteen AH-64 Apache helicopters first crossed the Iraqi border on January 17, 1991, soon to fire the first missiles of the Gulf War, only three out of the thirty-six men onboard had ever fired the real Hellfire missiles they were carrying.[7] In its very first issue, *Wired* published an enthusiastic article on this subject: "Most of the means of human perception in modern vehicles of war are already electronically mediated. In Desert Storm, both air pilots and tank crews spent much of their time in combat watching infrared targeting scopes. Much the same goes for Patriot missile crews, Aegis cruisers, AWACS radar personnel, and so on. War has become a phenomenon that America witnesses through screens. And it is a simple matter to wire those screens to present any image desired. Real tanks can engage simulator crews on real terrain which is also simultaneously virtual. Fake threats can show up on real radar screens, and real threats on fake screens."[8]

Seen from this angle, the Gulf War proved a very significant laboratory for all this technology, and gave rise to numerous specialized studies. This brief conflict, characterized by a disproportionate number of Iraqi casualties,[9] puts the idea of "information war" in perspective: the Gulf War was one of the first large-scale applications of the theory of "zero death." This theory, which attempts to create combat situations where the risk of harm to personnel is reduced, via accumulated information, to nothing is totally unrealistic in most types of engagement, modern or not; many if not most still are characterized by a domination of the weak by the strong, by rapacity, cruelty, and horror. During the Gulf War the theory could never be truly tested, given the tremendous gap in relative strength between the Iraqis and their opponents. What's more, the desert was a perfect staging ground for such a large-scale endeavor, launched, for the most part, from a "safe distance," well beyond range of most Iraqi weapons.

The information war buildup goes on. France sent its first spy satellite into orbit in July 1995. Named *Hélios* and launched from Kourou, Guyana, the satellite puts France in the technological big leagues. Now, they're drowning in remarkably detailed information, much like their American counterparts, who can review only 1% to 10% of all the images gathered: there is simply too much of it to analyze.

So what does this technology amount to? Are the French made more powerful by virtue of this gadgetry and its products? American strategist Edward Luttwak, a former CIA agent who now works at the Center for Strategic and International Studies (CSIS), where he leads discussion on the subject of the CIA's use of economic espionage, was perhaps being deliberately contentious when he first called for the various democracies to supply the Bosnians with arms and munitions.[10] But he was absolutely on target when he noted: "With their much larger populations, but much smaller families, none of today's advanced countries will sustain significant combat casualties, merely to resist aggressions against third parties. That leaves their armed forces in a peculiar situation: as interested as ever in obtaining the highest possible budgets, perhaps even more interested in expensively drilling and training to keep up a 'high rate of readiness, but entirely unready to fight against aggressors with a reputation for fighting back effectively.'"[11]

Despite the rapid rise of technological wizardry, war in all its ancient brutality seems likely to endure. Technologically advanced forces—those that futurologist Alvin Toffler classes in the "third wave"[12]—came up short in Somalia and the ex-Yugoslavia, Chechnia, and other hot spots around the globe. Nonetheless, the world's various forces relentlessly prepare for an information war that will eventually unfold and that offers advantages despite the recent shortfalls.

First of all, the "virtual" enemies are more active

than the real ones. For them war involves none of the cumbersome logistics of troop mobilization: all they need is a good cup of coffee and their computer keyboard to storm the beaches. Another advantage of information war (where nobody dies) is that it usually unfolds on an economic battlefield, where the major powers have expressed their rivalry since the collapse of Soviet Communism. If we take, as evidence of Zaki Laïdi's suggestion "that war is unthinkable between the democratic nations,"[13] the fact that for the first time in centuries we have no current conflicts between sovereign states, the most recent taking place in 1995 between Peru and Ecuador in a brief series of violent skirmishes, we must understand that war has been neither abolished nor forgotten. Since 1945, twenty-five large-scale armed conflicts have each led to at least one thousand deaths per year (and a half-million in 1994 in Rwanda alone).[14] The various industrialized nations as well as the United Nations have been powerless in limiting wars over issues of religion, nationalism, or territorial desire. That many of these conflicts have originated in areas where different groups had before lived together in peace seems to make no difference: massacres take place, armies use rape as a weapon, families are ripped apart, communities are traumatized, cities and land are destroyed, and human rights are violated by madmen and butchers.

Despite the explosion of high-tech planetary surveillance by the major industrialized nations, regional warfare isn't being stopped by the existence of the Internet, nor is it plausible to believe that it will have any great impact any time soon. Brute force still serves those who place little value on human life and free speech. But for the time being, according to Alvin Toffler, Newt Gingrich's good friend, the so-called advanced societies have other worries: "Third wave 'postnations,' of course, still need energy and food, but what they also need now is knowledge convertible into wealth. They need access to, or control of, world data banks and telecommunication networks. They need markets for intelligence-intensive products and services, for financial services . . . management consulting . . . software . . . television programming . . . banking . . . reservation systems . . . credit information . . . insurance . . . pharmaceutical research . . . network management . . . information systems integration . . . economic intelligence . . . training systems . . . simulations . . . news services . . . and all the information and telecommunications technologies on which they depend. They need protection against piracy of intellectual products."[15]

The Military on the Move

Contemporary capitalism is moving at lightning speed by virtue of the Internet and is showing no signs of slowing down, thanks, at least in part, to the Net's original developer, the U.S. military. But such rapid expansion and development has dictated certain changes. Although the Pentagon and DARPA (Defense Advanced Research Project Agency) founded the Net with ARPANET in 1969, its rapid popularization has meant that the network could no longer be used for the communication of America's most sensitive materials, coded or not. They kept ARPANET for research and offered the now defunct NSFnet for civil use.

A new, specialized global network has been put in place by the CIA for the exclusive use of its information services. In operation since December 1994, Interlink is considered so impenetrable that the jewels of the CIA's virtual crown are kept there: digital images collected by NRO (National Reconnaissance Office) spy satellites. The Pentagon's Internet addresses (all of which end in ".mil") are reserved for trivial bits of information and are available along the poorly protected Milnet.[16] For all confidential e-mails, the Internet is off limits: the Pentagon has its own Web.[17] Each homepage bears the same warning: "Security and Privacy Notice 1. This site is provided as a public service by the U.S. Army's Director of Information Systems for Command, Control, Communications and Computers (DISC4). 2. It is intended to be used by the public for viewing and retrieving information only. 3. Unauthorized attempts to upload or change information on this service are strictly prohibited and may be punishable under the Computer Fraud and Abuse act of 1986. 4. Statistics and other information about your visit are recorded. 5. All information on this site is considered public information and may be distributed and copied."

As history speeds forward, the Pentagon is one of the prime movers in information war, what they call "cyberwar." Not generally known as strategic theory virtuosos, even the Marines are on the lookout for new threats that could affect them during maneuvers. The development of the cellular telephone and its use by narcorevolutionaries in South America has been the subject of much military debate,[18] even though the limits of such technology have become clear. (The massive diffusion of Internet messages by Mexican guerrillas in Chiapas was soon mixed with an equally large number of fake messages and pieces of misinformation jeopardizing the public relations campaign of subcommander Marcos.)

During a symposium in Washington on June 6, 1995, Arthur Cebrowski, director of C^4 (Command, Control, Communication, and Computers), the senior oversight agency for the combined American Armed forces, estimated that it cost $1 billion in 1996 to keep American military computers safe. Based on the possibility of an "electronic Pearl Harbor" involving massive attacks by a group of hackers led by an enemy power, he explained the evolving mentality that sees a shift away from the threat of conventional nuclear assaults that terrified the Cold War world toward worries over a virtual Armageddon, fears that are understandable. You can see the rest of the argument coming from a mile away: military budgets may even increase as a result of this new threat.

This question of security has made those in charge develop new computerized military networks, designed expressly for the information age. The military, just like the rest of us, increasingly is communicating electronically but with a higher priority on security. The U.S. military uses more than 2.1 million computers, 10,000 local networks, and 100 long-distance networks.[19] In a study commissioned by the Rand Corporation, the authors noted that the growth of military networks forces a total reevaluation of American military strategy. Among many other considerations, they note: "Information warfare has no front line. Potential battlefields are anywhere networked systems allow access. Current trends suggest that the U.S. economy will increasingly rely on complex, interconnected network control systems for such necessities as oil and gas pipelines, electric grids, etc. The vulnerability of these systems is currently poorly understood. In addition, the means of deterrence and retaliation are uncertain and may rely on traditional military instruments in addition to information warfare threats. In sum, the U.S. homeland may no longer provide a sanctuary from outside attack."[20]

According to the Defense Information Systems Agency (DISA), which manages all Pentagon networks, American military computers were attacked an estimated 325,000 times in 1995, out of which only one in one hundred and fifty was detected and reported on. "Numerous defense functions have been adversely affected, including weapons and supercomputer research, logistics, finance, procurement, personnel management, military health and payroll."[21] All of these considerations must be taken into account as the U.S. military plans the global architecture of electronic communications of the future. In 1996 DISA built an operations center called the Global Operations and Security Center which is supposed to allow it to centralize information on all attacks on the Department of Defense while allowing the Pentagon to get a handle on the important data. Moreover, at the network infrastructure level, an enormous initiative named DISN

Support Services-Global, budgeted at $2 billion, has been given to Boeing to execute. In the coming years, the network named C⁴I (Command, Control, Communication, Computers, Intelligence) will allow the Pentagon to share "voice, data, video and messages systems, while providing security."[22] According to the Mission Need Statement put forward by DISA in October 1996, "The capability that provides transport of this mission critical C⁴I information must be global and seamless in connectivity, scaleable in capacity, flexible in provisioning, easily extended to any location in the world, and capable of accepting technology inserts and value added services in support of future warfighting requirements."[23]

When appointed CIA director on May 10, 1995, John Deutch gave much thought to these issues. He established an interagency think tank charged with defining the improvements necessary to private and governmental telecommunications security, as well as computer networks ("Everybody says it is a huge problem and will cost billions of dollars to fix. But they don't tell you more about it after that"):[24] a call to putting all the issues on the table for discussion, even if no quick resolution is at hand.

Until now, there's been little to justify these worries, although the Pentagon has confirmed several ferocious attacks by hackers and openly admits fearing the introduction of viruses into its servers. They also admit, however, that these attacks have been made against their weakest systems, like Milnet, which aren't equipped with any serious protection and hold no sensitive information. The questions remain: how have hackers penetrated military computers in the past? how are they entering them now? Details of such intrusions have been swallowed up by the Pentagon out of a desire to minimize the attacks and keep attention away from weak spots in their network or to make them seem more important in the eyes of the public, which would help them justify their budget. A recent attack on CIA's Web site by Swedish hackers in 1996 is an interesting example. The gambit was a source of embarrassment to the CIA, but no vital information was ever at risk. In the GAO report mentioned earlier (see note 19), analysts underlined that the attacks against the U.S. Air Force's Rome (New York) Laboratory in March and April of 1994 by a British hacker were a completely different problem, and may have been undertaken with criminal intentions: "Air force officials told us that at least one of the hackers may have been working for a foreign country interested in obtaining military research data. . . . In addition, the hackers may have intended to install malicious code in software which could be activated years later, possibly jeopardizing a weapon system's ability to perform safely and as intended, and even threatening the lives of the soldiers or pilots operating the system."[25]

The Pentagon's willingness in the best of times to confront worst-case scenarios has made them put things into high gear. In February 1994, the Automated Systems Security Incident Support Team (ASSIST) was formed, specializing in the treatment of incidents provoked by hackers. ASSIST was entrusted to its ad hoc agency, the Center for Information Systems Security (CISS), and given technical input by the NSA working closely with the National Computer Security Center (NCSC). During a colloquium in Washington in 1994 devoted to the threats posed by computer delinquency to American security, Scott Charney, chief of the Computer Crimes Unit (CCU), a branch of the Justice Department, sounded the alarm. The big worry seems to be that hackers could be tempted away from their computer hijinks and into the lucrative employ of criminal organizations: "In the past, information was put in a safe, which was then locked. We locked the building, put a fence around it, and put in guards to make sure [the information] was safe. Now, we put sensitive information on line, and rest comfortably because there's a fence around the building."[26]

American military officials are earmarking a lot of money for fighting the virtual intruders in the name of the safety of the United States and its citizens. And since the best defense is a good offense, it would not be surprising to see the United States in the role of attacker, corrupting hostile systems with viruses and logic bombs. One way or another, for the immediate future at least, it seems that there will be a lot of work for hackers.

8
The Internet and Espionomics

Don't mention the Internet to Airbus Industries: they can't stand it. They believe that their major competitor, Boeing, uses the Internet to attack them. It all started after an excerpt from the accident report relating to the crash of an Absheim A-320 on June 25, 1988, appeared over the Internet. The accident, caused by a risky flight demonstration at an air show, killed four and wounded one hundred. The problem with the excerpt's appearance was that the report from which it was taken had not yet been made public, and the parts of it that defended Airbus's actions were creatively edited out. Then, suddenly, hostile messages against Airbus and its French partner, Aérospatiale, began mysteriously appearing in newsgroups devoted to aeronautics and transportation.

The Internet: The Perfect Tool for Misinformation

Several enthusiastic Aérospatiale officials were also expert Websurfers and had been watching the newsgroups with interest. One reason was that they enjoyed them, but another was that Aérospatiale had been one of the early companies to understand that these groups were a "practical means of identifying experts in their industry and of evaluating competition in new technologies and markets."[1] But officials were surprised by the virulence of the attacks they observed, so they began tracking the messages back to their authors. Without much difficulty, they figured out the addresses of origin and the common nodes across the globe through which the messages had been sent. Unfortunately, upon closer inspection, all the addresses and their wrappers turned out to be fake, easy enough to manage for those who know UNIX. The messages were really coming from the United States, with fabricated wrappers generated by anonymous servers in Finland. Based on analysis of the wrappers, Aérospatiale strongly suspected Boeing had just launched one of the first big campaigns of misinformation on the Internet.

Newsgroups, however, aren't only useful as means of attack: businesses can also use them to gather information. Another example from the world of aeronautics: after the crash of an ATR aircraft[2] in the United States on Halloween, 1994, their entire fleet was grounded for two months during the ensuing investigation. In financial terms, the decision was catastrophic—two months of lost revenue. During the grounding, debate over the situation raged in specialized newsgroups, including CompuServe's AVSIG.

Statements in favor of the European builders of the plane were few and well outnumbered on the Internet by statements against them. One day in January 1995, an inconspicuous message appeared from a journalist writing for a specialized aeronautics regulation publication: "I heard that the flight restrictions are going to be lifted. Could someone please confirm?" Which someone soon did. Then, just three days later, the official decision that they could fly again was handed down to ATR. Had they been following newsgroup discussions, they would have gotten a three-day jump on things.

Newsgroups have become yet another source for the gathering of economic intelligence. Knowing what events might have specific consequences for the life of a company or a country has begun to justify the massive expenditures that make the accumulation of such information possible. Whether or not it is true, as many have asserted, that the economy has become the new battlefield for democratic nations, it is certain that in today's business environments, access to information is making and breaking companies and that the Internet has become the essential means to such ends.

Another French firm that had to deal with a negative Internet campaign against it was the petroleum giant Total. Total was preparing to tap into a huge undersea natural gas deposit in Burma. The French had invested heavily in a refinery on Burmese soil, but there was a problem: Aung San Suu Kyi, Nobel Peace Prize winner and defender of the rights of the Burmese people, was opposed to the project on the grounds that it would only line the pockets of the antidemocratic military junta she and her followers had long been fighting. She de-

manded a halt to the project and a departure of Total from Burma, an entirely reasonable stance. Nelson Mandela had made similar demands of various
companies while fighting against apartheid. On various Internet newsgroups (like soc.culture.burma),
as well as on various nongovernmental militant
sites, including that of planetary speculator George
Soros,[3] Total was called every name in the book,
deluged in a Internet opinion tsunami. Total contacted the International Federation of the Rights of
Man (FIDH) and tried to show them and the rest of
the world that they were exploiting no one and that
their investments would help the Burmese people
not hurt them. Total paid the plane fare for numerous French and world journalists to visit Burma
and see first hand that all was well. Naturally, there
was little newsworthy to see. Internet-savy consul-
tants took the Total/Burma incident as a test case
and designed counterstrategies for the firm, going
so far as to launch an autonomous counteroffensive
based on their belief that the opposition to Total was
an Anglo-Saxon conspiracy to oust the firm from
Burma. The reality of the situation was considerably more complex. In March 1997, debate raged in
the U.S. Congress over what stance to take toward
Burma: should economic ties be broken? Should
the United States follow France and continue to
court investment in Burma? The same political
slugfest that surrounded South Africa under
apartheid raged again, but with more spectators
around, and in, a ring that was now accessible to
anyone with a modem and a computer, for better or
for worse.

Information: Secret Weapon

Who filed the most recent patent on polymers? What team did the researcher belong to and is he planning on staying there? What trips did the former Russian foreign minister Andrei Kozirev take prior to 1985? Who are the foremost experts on aeronautic stealth technology? What can we expect from the Brazilian automobile market from now until the end of the century? The answers to such questions are all available in digital form and can be worth fortunes to those who need immediate access to them.

Today, information is a weapon: and it is available in over five thousand online databases in the United States and around the world. Filled with millions of pages of doctoral theses, treatises on every subject imaginable, scientific publications from all corners of the world, these databases have become an extraordinary storehouse of human knowledge. Most of these documents can be located with search engines such as Yahoo, which can look throughout the vast networks by using key words or full text. For a fee the biggies like Dialog and Lexis/Nexis will release contents of tens of thousands of publications. It's increasingly rare for the top international publications to be unavailable online as well as on paper, particularly since it costs them so little: the articles are already written and on computer. Consulting articles on these databases are billed from a dollar to a few dollars per text, so major research will cost you. Though these information banks have been around for a while, their full potential has yet to be exploited. The secret services were the first to take an interest in these supremely complex sorting programs that are able to manipulate databases in order to extract and analyze information available in them.

It's not at all surprising that the CIA has led the way. They've invested heavily in these systems. Their goal has been to treat as much raw data as possible in the least amount of time, extracting those sensitive details unavailable elsewhere. DARPA, the Pentagon agency involved in the earliest days of the Internet, launched the first studies on this subject during the seventies. Early, only brief, simple messages and internal memos were addressed; later the wire reports from news agencies were automatically distributed to all relevant parties. Then, as things progressed, they began treating the mass of information available on databases, attempting to pioneer convenient, time-saving means of rapid search. Topic is one of the "search engines" that came out of this period, and quickly became an industry standard for database research.[4] Though initially available only to the military and the secret services, Topic soon became an essential research tool, integrated into the software of numerous companies.

For those who deal in large quantities of incoming information, doing without search engines has become inconceivable. The Atomic Energy Commission developed software that addressed its specific needs. Called Sprint, it is able to manage texts in various languages and to sort them automatically. Another example of network research analysis software is Taiga, developed for France's DGSE by Christian Krumeich at Thomson computer. It was originally designed as a means of searching databases concerning the former Soviet Union. Only recently has Taiga been approved for nongovernmental use, running about forty thousand dollars a pop and now owned and developed by the Madicia company. Madicia was bought by Questel, a subsidiary of France Télécom. In the spring of 1995, Questel tried to sell Madicia to IBM for about $1 million, but public opinion rallied against the sale and helped kill the deal in the name of nationalism. Taiga was finally sold to IPSIC, which renamed Taiga Noemic. Noemic is used most by the DRM (direction du renseignement militaire), which seems thoroughly pleased with it.

Noemic/Taiga is able to merge data automatically and can handle texts in any language, whether located in databases or arriving from the news services. If a Taiga user is interested in cultivating peppers, the program can be used to automatically search for and sort all available Internet information, as well as information from news agencies and articles in databases. It is able to wrangle tough semantic and linguistic impediments; it doesn't crash at the sight of parataxis or anaphora; it easily juggles tropes, skips through diachronies, and laughs at hapax legomenon.[5] Thanks to the work of a young Corsican programmer, Pascal Andréi, Taiga's repertoire was further expanded to include technological analysis in addition to its initial geopolitical focus. It works on the basis of translating (automatically) all texts to be analyzed into a metalanguage which will then be analyzed by the program. Take this hypothetical example of a message Taiga might receive: "An Airbus A-320 was en route to Asia. An explosion onboard took place somewhere above Tripoli. The Algerian defense minister was killed." In the blink of an eye (at the speed of one billion characters per second), the program translates this into pivot language as follows: "be-tch-dpl-air/cmc/airb/a320, be-loc-pol-vil/cap/lby, ag-phy-vlc, bpp/bpf-min-def\alg." Taiga has its own lexicon from which this equivalent is composed: An Airbus A-320 is translated into the broad category of "technological thing" (be-tech), "moving in the air" (dpl-air), "commercial" (cmc); an explosion becomes "to act physically with violence" (ag-phy-vlc), and so forth.

Thanks to its mastery of linguistic subtleties (metaphors, circumlocutions), Taiga is able to make sense not just of words but of progressions of ideas. With Taiga, key words are unnecessary: Terms defined in the pivot language are regrouped by common concepts (airplane and helicopter), which a classic key word (either plane or helicopter) wouldn't have included. In the previous example, references to the two machines could have been found under a search for be-tech-dpl-air.

Pascal Andréi never tires of explaining how his little marvel works: "It all boils down to starting with good dictionaries to get an understanding of the specific terms used in the domain one is going to study. Although some good dictionaries are available, for the most part we compile them ourselves." To do this, it's often necessary to resort to techniques used in the world of artificial intelligence, calling in cognicians who "download" the expertise of specialists into Taiga. As such, building on our pepper cultivation example, a gardening specialist would need to be interviewed to create a metalanguage dictionary for our pepper search with a glossary of terms that will make for a fruitful search.

This is sometimes seen as a liability by naysayers, some at the DGSE, who feel that Taiga is too complicated. Others say that while Taiga represented a very interesting solution in the early nineties, its competitors have since surpassed it. But for those who learn how to use it, Taiga is a most powerful tool. At the end of 1996, Christian Krumeich began to sell an updated version of Taiga, called Noemic, that uses yet more sophisticated semantic manipulations.

If France's DGSE is still having some difficulty watching over the entirety of the network and its information, it can't be faulted for lack of effort. The French are most interested in newsgroups, and software specializing in "enhanced information" is already in use to manage the flow of important digital communications—even digital telephone conversations intercepted legally or not, digitized and translated into pivot language. This is not as far-fetched as it may first seem. After a television exposé in January 1994, an official of the German BND admitted that their COMPINT unit had been specializing in computer intelligence. During the same period, it was learned that the BND had figured out how to bolster its lexical databases, which allowed them to automatically listen in and analyze intercepted telephone conversations.

In early 1995, the French DRM bought several dozen Taiga stations. Running software much like that employed by the NSA, the DRM expanded mightily on its ability to automatically listen in and analyze the Internet. Take the example of two

CompuServe customers living in Paris; if one sends an e-mail to the other, the message always passes through a node in Columbus, Ohio, where Compu-Serve has its major installation. Therefore electronic communications that are actually local may really be international and, on passing through the United States, will give the NSA more of an opportunity to intercept them.

For those interested in information analysis the Internet is a rainbow leading to a pot of gold. The promoters of the development of Taiga-like software believe that huge quantities of economic activity, heretofore inaccessible, will soon become transparent to surveillance in such domains as strategic information, surveillance technology, and economic information. Such access will become a source for incredible wealth for specialists working legally within businesses (or illegally, for some companies), or secret services. By setting up batteries of information filters and semantic analysis processes, we can automatically create new information out of these raw chunks of data.

Thomson computer, one of the original developers of Taiga, runs the CIA's Topic on its network devoted to surveillance technology, GRIT. As explained in a promotional brochure for the Verity company, which distributes the CIA's program, Topic can sort through twenty to thirty thousand new documents per month drawn from databases and arriving via CD-ROM and magnetic tape: "Each subscriber to this service receives a monthly selection of summaries that corresponds to their areas of interest. These summaries, called research profiles, are strictly defined in advance by the researcher in charge of the selective issuing of information." A big armaments company would be delighted to have an efficient means of keeping its engineers up to date on the latest-breaking news in its industry, wherever it might be. The CIA's software developers' hard work has made Topic an industry standard, and more than ten thousand companies around the world use it. A new version, Topic WebSearcher, has been specially adapted to index and search information on the Internet. In this domain, those who develop the simplest, fastest interfaces will reap huge financial rewards. Another search engine called Yahoo[6] was put together by two very smart students, David Filo and Jerry Yang. Filo and Yang were both Ph.D. candidates in electrical engineering at Stanford University. In April 1994, they began to build their own database. Their goal was simply to tidy up their scattered interests across the Web so that they could more easily manipulate and navigate through it all. Little by little, their system grew bigger and bigger, and they began to develop software programs specifically dedicated to their needs and to those of thousands of websurfers who quickly came to depend on their services. As a result, Yahoo has become one of the prime engines used to search the World Wide Web, and found its place there around the same time as another program, Lycos,[7] developed by Carnegie-Mellon University. Operating on a higher conceptual plane, the Gingo program was developed at the TriVium company (headed by economist Richard Collin) by a multidisciplinary team close to Michel Serres, made up of Michel Authier, a mathmatician and sociologist, and the philosopher Pierre Lévy. Gingo is designed to "navigate through complicated information systems," and to "master the developing domain of the virtual economy." For example, when a company wishes to establish a map of the set of skills associated with its personnel, Ginko will create a graphical representation in the form of a knowledge tree on which each person is assigned a position and where all knowledge is represented in an immediately vizualized graphical form. Such programs allow visualization of constantly changing information that is constantly and automatically updated. This software allows companies to make more informed strategic decisions than ever before, based on a complexity of analysis hitherto unimaginable. Another system pioneered by the French is Pericles, developed by former Aeronavale pilots who launched a company called Datatops. Their programs are designed to analyze network information to the end of filtering it down to the bits of gold essential to their clients. Their program began to have some commercial success in 1996 thanks to positive word of mouth. But many other companies are vying for a share of this new market. The California company Semio, a venture uniting Frenchman Claude Vogel and American Stecen Gal, introduced Semiomap in February 1997, a search engine that represents its information through a powerful graphic interface that links words and images. These tools have launched new careers like those in the making at Psytep in Corpus Christi, Texas. Using Delfin's Infopower program, Psytep prepares reports for various companies, giving them detailed pictures of their unique competitive environments and allowing the companies to better adapt and compete.

Another American program, DR-LINK (Document Retrieval through Linguistic Knowledge), is manufactured by Textwise, a company founded by Mike Weiner, formerly of Rank-Xerox, and Elisabeth Liddy, a computer scientist from Syracuse University. Their program allows the extraction of information from digital databases, wherever they may be. ARPA, which long ago first financed the Internet, also funded the development of this program through Tipster, an initiative launched by the information-gathering community. Each system has its own specifications and particular strengths, but that hasn't stopped the onslaught of new programs from entering the market. There seems to be a new piece of software every week, and an inventory of these tools wouldn't be complete without mentioning Netowl and NameTag, launched by SRA International and Isoquest.

Each of these systems can address the proliferating number of servers connected around the world, index their contents, and analyze daily any added information, thus allowing users to access the latest information. Estimates of the total global number of Web sites are bound to be imprecise. But Matthew Gray, a researcher at MIT, gave the following approximations in his "Internet Growth Summary" of 1996: June 1995, 23,600 sites; January 1996, 100,000 sites; June 1996, 230,000 sites; and January 1997, 650,000 sites—a twenty-fold growth in twelve months![9] Each system can recognize nearly all the Web servers around the globe and index and analyze the dozens of new venues that emerge daily so that users can find their way to them. The engines available on the Internet illustrate the network's extraordinary power and make abundantly clear that a new age has arrived: information that would have taken days or weeks in a library can now be accessed effortlessly, instantly, and in greater depth and quantity than ever before. It isn't that our libraries will go the way of Alexandria: they aren't necessarily endangered species. But it is clear that their role will change. Libraries will soon be virtual structures, accessible via the Internet.

Of course, there are bound to be difficulties, even if those difficulties arise out of apparent advancements. Take the search engine that appeared in early 1996, Dejanews. The engine is able to seek out single words or names in the totality of newsgroups on the Internet. The engine is fast, efficient, and reliable. If you wanted information on your neighbor, within a few seconds Dejanews could search through months of chat sessions and list every occurrence of the name. Then, and this is where things get scary, by clicking on his name, you could find statistics on how often he logged on, his favorite subjects, those in which he participates, and those messages to which he responds. Another mechanism found in many search engines is called a "magic cookie." A magic cookie gives a server information it deems useful about its clients. This information might include the time of logon, the chat rooms visited, the amount of time spent there, the user's type of computer, even the names of the user's software. With this information, the server can then forward advertisements and promotions he feels are suited to a client. Furthermore, this information can be sold to companies or service providers with the hope that they can direct-market to a receptive prescreened potential buyer. As a result, huge files of behavioral information are constantly compiled about those who log on. Although this sounds straight out of Orwell, it's not all bad news: happily, the Net being what it is (a self-policing utopia), cyber–fairy godmothers have created "cookie monsters" that keep these magic cookies from collecting in the wrong jars.

Surprisingly, use of these search engines is free. As travelers on the Internet are so dependent on the functionality of these engines, one might expect them to cost a bundle to use, particularly when they represent the only means of access to information that may be lodged half a world away on a computer in a foreign university. This sort of free exchange of information is just what has made everyone so excited about the Internet and so hopeful that the information superhighway might lead us to a new era of personal freedom. Unfortunately, it seems that the superhighway is about to become a toll road, or so some companies hope.

Enhanced Information: A User's Guide

The French are very involved with enhanced information and have dedicated a part of their FBI, the DST, to the development of this "industry." The DST periodically organizes a colloquium where the 150 French specialists involved in the industry meet for one week to discuss the latest news in their field. The information presented at their latest gathering, May 30 to June 2, 1995, drew the attention of the world's largest corporations, many of whom sent representatives to the conference: Rhone-Poulenc, Aérospatiale, Commissariat à l'énergie atomique, EDF (Électricité de France), IBM, L'Oréal, Synthélabo, Michelin, and others.

To better understand the usefulness of *information elaborée*, we can look at this example. Say a chemical company team of specialists studying infrared microscope technology wants some information. Sitting down at their office computer (the hard drive of which might contain a program like Dataview, a search engine developed by a research institute), they log onto the Internet and access an American database called Chemical Abstracts, which contains references to 15 million articles on chemistry. The company wants to know who else is doing research in their very specialized high-tech domain. By using their search engine they can look first for articles dealing with infrared technology and then narrow it down to those whose work is most similar to theirs. Research has never been easier or more potentially thorough.

Bernard Dousset of the IRIT in Toulouse, France, contributed to the development of an astonishing piece of software, Tétralogie. For those who consult databases frequently, it's not at all unusual, when researching a scientific topic, for five thousand to ten thousand documents to be analyzed at a time. The analysis begins with a search across the Internet for databases most applicable to the search. Then, very quickly, the rough data begin to take the form of multidimensional graphs that appear on workstation screens. In the world of science, dialogue between researchers at symposia is as much the lifeblood of research as the articles in scientific journals. Often, these articles seem to be miniature symposia, as they are often written by a group of researchers rather than an individual. Learning the names of those in a given field, correlating and bringing them together, and analyzing their sundry connections is the main function of Tétralogie. After Tétralogie processes the data it color-codes everything and everyone, assigns each researcher a single point, and gathers the colors into groups. These then can be manipulated to see, in vivid visuals, who has been working together, who has been working alone, and who might be tempted over to your group. Bernard Dousset explains a sample screen: "What we see here, clearly, are the mandarins of this field. Those who hold onto their workers and don't let them go elsewhere. And those who move around and work for everyone. It's not much more complicated than that; before a symposium, if you study the chart, you can see in about two minutes who are the four or five researchers you want to pursue."

Officially, explains Touafiq Dkaki at the IRIT Web site,[10] "the information used to piece together the collaboration networks comes from bibliographically structured databases. These formal networks allow us to discover hidden alliances, to detect isolated research teams, and to understand the progress of technology." More prosaically, a skilled user will be able to root out malcontents and embittered members of the scientific community, those who might be receptive to offers from other quarters, as well as those who might not. Without much difficulty, Tétralogie can even discover the "invisible" colleagues of a given group that the bigwigs are trying to hang onto, "which you can spot when names appear where they shouldn't." Clearly, the purpose of this software is to gather information, more precisely, competitive information. "This involves a series of steps which begins with the collection of information and ends with the making of a decision."[11] Whether for companies or spies (or the two rolled into one), Tétralogie has become a useful tool in persuading experts to join one's ranks.

Other software programs have been developed that offer different possibilities. For specialists it's all about being able to get the gist of a given server or database as quickly as possible or to ferret through all the conversations of a given newsgroup. The program Sprint automatically indexes huge quantities of online information (fifty megaoctets or thirty-three thousand pages in five minutes). These texts are drawn from structural text databases comprising short "abstracts" about the work of their authors or from "structurals," containing raw data (chemical equations, factual scientific data). Developed with the assistance of experts in linguistics, these specialized software programs search words newly added to databases, as well as those old words used less and less or disappearing altogether. Through this precise semantic analysis, emerging technologies can be predicted by the frequency of use of their new technological terms. In the same way, technologies on the wane can be flagged by a decreasing number of references to them. Other tools such as TWatch (Technology Watch) developed by IBM-France allow economic information gathering on a large scale. Some can search and sort the juiciest sources available on the Internet, the patent databases.

Some programs are developed for the specific needs of a client. When the French Ministry of the Interior needed a custom program, it called upon the French firm Language Naturel SA to develop Messie (messiah, in English). Specializing in message routing, Messie analyzes message contents before dividing them among different departments of the national police. The recipients don't need to indicate key words that they wish to find in a text. Based on the prior analysis of definitions in a business dictionary, Messie creates a "semantic network" that eliminates all the semantic problems.

In an open document, France's SGDN (Secretary General of National Defense) compared the functionality of several enhanced information programs. It noted that Topic, despite its incredibly high performance, is too difficult to customize, and Taïga requires the building of customized lexicons covering the fields which the software has not yet encountered. It concluded that despite some very real, very notable successes, there was still progress to be made: "The parts of the software most in need of development involve both the performance of linguistic processing modules and the construction of field-specific lexicons. In order to achieve systems that maximize the processing of text-based information, the development of these lexicons is essential."

My, What Big Ears You Have

There's a very thin line between economic "espionage" and economic "intelligence." This so-called intelligence, if we use Christian Harbulot's definition, consists of the "search and systematic interpretation of information accessible to everyone, with, as its objective, learning the intentions and capacities of those involved. It encompasses all aspects of surveillance of the competitive environment."[12]

In the United States, the archetype for the private gathering of information is Wackenhut Corporation, a security firm founded by George Wackenhut. He had his fifteen minutes of fame in the early nineties for executing a few little jobs for the CIA and the federal government. During an investigation by the Department of Energy into Westinghouse, a major builder of nuclear reactor components, the dubious methods used by Wackenhut Corporation came to light. Wackenhut had installed 147 telephone tap systems into Westinghouse and a few other companies. Some of the systems were so powerful that they could handle as many as two hundred separate conversations simultaneously.

Many companies, most of which are in the United States, specialize in high-end economic intelligence in addition to their basic security services and strategic consulting services. Kroll Associates[13] is the best known and most important of these, along with Fuld & Co,[14] Kirk Tyson International,[15] Parvus, Futures Group, and a few others. The near future will surely see the entry of many more competitors in this emerging market. According to the confidential *Intelligence Newsletter* published by Indigo Publications,[16] in the near future large accounting firms like Coopers and Lybrand, Deloitte and Touche, and Arthur Andersen, which are a part of the "Big Six" along with Ernst and Young, KPMG–

Peat Marwick, and Price Waterhouse, will tiptoe into the pool.[17] Since these accounting firms are American, this will do nothing to decrease the tension between developing nations arising from increasingly ferocious economic competition. Already, the Big Six have come to dominate accounting in Europe, and their operations allow them to gather very priviledged information about those clients they currently serve. And the idea that these same companies would soon be selling their services as hunter-gatherers of economic information has worried more than a few Europeans: "Some European nations are concerned over the strategic implications of the trend which could see the United States and Britain, via the Big Six, gaining an ever-tighter grip on worldwide business intelligence and penetrating local markets which have so far remained beyond their grasp. For years France's DST has been warning about the danger of Big Six firms pillaging French corporate secrets. The government has now given every sign of being ready to react by throwing its support behind what it considers a 'sound French alternative' in the field of consultancy and business intelligence."[18]

The best-known information companies say this sort of thing is absolutely off-limits. Jean-Claude Chalumeau, a Harvard graduate and head of the Paris office of Kroll Associates (founded by Jules Kroll, a New York lawyer), recruited Yves Bauemlin, a former DST counterespionage chief, to work for them. The DST caught wind of the hiring and was furious: it's one thing when their former employees go to work for French companies, but for a foreign company? Chalumeau says that hiring the former

DST man made sense and that it was the best way to organize the gathering of "human source" information. In January 1997, Bauemlin finally replaced Chalumeau, who resigned after a disagreement over what direction Kroll France should take. When the office opened, 20% of the information they processed was human in origin, and the other 80% originated in online databases. But the lion's share of their activity remains oriented toward economic information gathering for the good of clients who pay them quite well for their work: three thousand dollars a day. But the game is worth it. Information collected by Jules Kroll can be what makes or breaks a business, so who cares what it costs? Companies call on Kroll to discover the strategic intentions of their competitors and sometimes to negotiate ransom to be paid for a worker who has been kidnapped in the Third World. Kroll is proud of some other accomplishments: he tracked the administrators of Saddam Hussein's fortune across the world—$11 billion diverted from his country's petroleum revenues and with which he bought up companies all over Europe and the United States.

In the United States and Canada, threats by foreign powers against companies within both countries are perceived as threats to their national interests. In Canada the SCSR (Canadian Security and Information Service)[19] created a structure specializing in giving advice to companies about counterespionage techniques in an effort to remedy the laxity in such situations. The U.S. government provides information to businesses by giving them access to the State Department's BBS. In electronic form, companies can receive daily updates from the Office of Intelligence and Threat Analysis offering a world-wide catalog of hot spots where Americans are at risk and where local political and economic conditions are unstable.

In 1992 the FBI expanded its purview for investigations to include potential "threats" that don't, in the narrowest sense threaten the United States' strategic interests, by setting up a national security checklist. This list was used in legal proceedings taken against the Ames Research Center in Mountain View, California, which was accused of not protecting top secret information (including files related to contracts with NASA) with the degree of care the FBI would have wished.[20]

Another list, the Military Critical Technology List (MCTL), was published in 1996. The list consists of twenty-six technologies most vital to to American interests, including almost everything that is cutting-edge.[21] American authorities finally decided to take radical measures to organize their fight against those who had been attacking U.S. firms. This major shift in the U.S. stance that occurred after the collapse of Communism and the Berlin wall embodies a clear desire to protect against new threats to security, but also an equal desire to reorganize existing counterespionnage around a new challenge. The new National Counterintelligence Policy Board (NACIPB) was created in 1994 by the Presidential Decision Directive NSC-24 and serves as "an inter-agency organization staffed with counterintelligence and security professionals from the FBI, CIA, NSA, DIA, and the Departments of Defense and State. The NACIC is primarily responsible for coordinating national-level counterintelligence activities, and reports to the National Security Council through the National Counterintelligence Policy Board (NACIPB)."[22] In 1994 the NACIC assures us, seventy-four American companies at home and abroad were subject to 446 illegal attempts at jeopardizing their economic interests. These incidents do not necessarily implicate foreign governments: the companies report that in only 16% of the incidents were the attacks conducted by other governments. The majority were incidents of industrial espionnage launched by rival firms. In its annual report of 1996, the NACIC didn't disclose the nations accused of conducting espionage against U.S. firms: the list is classified. Anonymous sources within the U.S. government confirm that close allies like France, South Korea, Japan, and Germany are all suspects in such matters. By current estimates the U.S. economy loses $2 billion per month to economic espionage, which more than explains all the retaliatory ardor.

9
Economics, the New Battlefield

When the Brazilian government wanted to reorganize the aerial surveillance of the Amazon it sent out a call for bids on the project. The promise of a $1.5 billion contract caught a lot of attention. The major U.S. weapons firm Raytheon put itself forward, as well as the European firms Thomson and Alcatel. Raytheon prevailed, using a new strategy that went beyond just having a more attractive proposal.

An American Offensive

As the U.S. undersecretary of commerce explained in January 1995, the Brazilian affair exemplifies the extent to which the U.S. government is now willing to help private enterprise win contracts and defeat international competitors. Bill Clinton himself was said to be in on the maneuvers that helped Raytheon win the day in Brazil, giving the company a $1.4 billion contract.

During the summer of 1994, when it appeared that the Brazilians were going to choose the French company Thomson for the job, emergency meetings were held every morning in Washington at eight o'clock. Participants included the president of Exim-bank, the president of OPIC (Overseas Private Investment Corporation), the heads of the EPA and the TDA (Trade and Development Agency), and high-ups from the NSC (National Security Council), the NEC (National Economic Council), and the State Department. During these gatherings, a strategy was established: first, the American proposals were adapted to be more in line with those of the French. Then a public relations campaign was launched against the French in Brazil, alleging that the French had bribed their way toward the contract. Once the announcement of the SIVAM agreement was made (July 24, 1994), Secretary of Commerce Ron Brown proclaimed: "Once again, it demonstrates the seriousness of purpose we have in standing shoulder to shoulder with American business and protecting the commercial interests of the United States."[1] In fact, rather rapidly, some serious accusations were leveled over how the United States had prevailed in the contractual maneuverings. In matters of money, however, it is rare for the good guys and the bad guys to line up neatly on opposite sides of the yellow line: corruption is a two-way street. Accusations of disloyalty leveled at the French were never substantiated. In fact it was the United States that would find itself in hot water a year and a half after the contracts had been signed. In November 1995, Raytheon was accused, within Brazil, of having bribed those who had doled out the contracts. Wiretap transcripts published in the Argentinian press implicated Gomez dos Santos (head of protocol for President Fernando Henrique Cardoso) and M. Assumpçao, Raytheon's Brazilian spokesperson. It was alleged that Assumpçao had bribed Gilberto Miranda, the liason to SIVAM for the Brazilian senate. The accusations caused political upheaval within Brazil.

In a similar situation, IBM was accused of rigging the conditions under which a contract was signed which won them the job of automating Argentina's National Bank in 1994. Worth $250 million, it was the biggest computer contract ever signed in Latin America. President Carlos Menem voided it, after serious charges of corruption had been leveled, staunching a flow of $32 million earmarked for governmental high-ups. During a Buenos Aires press conference on December 16, 1996, Dingo Cavallo, the former economic minister accused President Menem of knowing about the payouts.

Though bribery has never been proven in either case, they raise some interesting questions. As the German nongovernmental organization Transparency International declares: "While different societies may draw the line of acceptable conduct at differing levels, there is no country where the people consider it proper that those in positions of political power enrich themselves through illicit agreements with commercial contractors at the expense of the best interests of the citizenry. In such a system the bribe giver is as guilty as the bribe taker."[2]

Is it illegal for a company to pay a commission to a legal intermediary? Clearly any sort of payment becomes problematic when the intermediary is a political figure belonging to a ruling party. From the French point of view, this wasn't an issue; the French finance minister budgets for foreign com-

mercial expenses as long as they are made public
and amount to less than 15% of the total value of the
contract. This attitude is shared by most major
manufacturers the world over. Often, the formal
process of securing foreign bids hides a vast network
of corruption led by local bigwigs who transfer public funds into private pockets, all of which is con-
doned by the contractor who pays the bribes and
then overcharges for the whole deal by an amount
equivalent to the bribes.

Business and politics being what they are, the
United States isn't going to warm to the idea of a foreign power making major armaments deals in its
backyard or, for that matter, anywhere that its interests lie. With cuts to the Pentagon budget in recent years and the resulting loss of business to arms
manufacturers accustomed to high defense spending, it comes as no surprise that information war
could be adapted to commercial applications. Clearly, the U.S. government's information services were
of direct assistance to Raytheon, and the company
certainly wasn't hurt by Commerce Secretary Ron
Brown's official visit to Brazil.[3] Indeed, Raytheon's
president, Denis J. Piccard, was one of the members
of the delegation that accompanied him. This sort of
high-level, semiofficial brokering of deals has become something of a norm; it won Murphy Jahn-
Tams a $1 billion contract in Bangkok to build a new
airport, beating out the French firm Aéroports de
Paris.

It seems then that information services are
helping private companies indirectly and directly,
offering them insights into their competitors' strategies and sometimes intervening more dramatically.

Documents are stolen from hotel rooms; portable computer hard disks are copied; phone calls are recorded and information transmitted by modem is intercepted. There is no limit to what will be attempted in the pursuit of corporate secrets, including psychological warfare.

In the United States a debate rages around the issue. Some believe that the secret services should be using all means at their disposal to assist private enterprise, whereas others feel that the private and public sectors should be as distinct from each other as church and state.

The French began dealing with these issues in earnest after the FBI and the CIA caught their agents infiltrating IBM, Texas Instruments, and Corning Glass, as discussed earlier. The French have no compunction over using their information services to help their businesses, and the nationalization of most French manufacturing after the Second World War goes a long way toward explaining this comfortable symbiosis. Claude Silberzahn, head of France's DGSE, who brokered the accord between the United States and his country after France was caught red-handed, explains the changes that were coming to bear as the eighties drew to a close: "A major difference between the Americans and the French was (and may still be) that if the Americans had done as the French were doing, they would have betrayed their belief in a separation between public and private sectors. They would have been tinkering with their view of a market economy. This is the difference between purely liberal American society and the mixture of economic means to an end at work in France."[4] Despite the trend set by his predecessors at the DGSE, Silberzahn has been consistently against providing French companies with useful information about their competitors. He believes that the risk of hurting relations with an ally by trafficking such information is too great and that the DGSE's principal business should be to serve and protect the state.

Pierre Lacoste, a former head of the DGSE who had to resign after the Greenpeace affair,[5] also believed that the French secret services shouldn't run risks associated with trying to help domestic firms beat out those of foreign allies for contracts: "The desire to defend our country's varied interests should not be used to justify means which go beyond what is decent and right. If we want to help a French company trying to get a foreign contract, the secret services should not leave themselves open to accusations of unethical activities."[6]

In April 1992, CIA Director Robert Gates stated his opposition to economic espionage before Congress. But Stansfield Turner, his predecessor at the CIA from March 1977 to January 1981 was openly regretful over the attitude shared by his subordinates: "I made a big effort to get the intelligence community to support U.S. business. I was told by CIA professionals that this was not national security."[7]

Bill Clinton (whose predecessor was a former CIA chief) is very interested in this issue and seems to want to treat economic markets as aspects of foreign policy. When first elected, Clinton created the NEC, which quickly began to work alongside the information-gathering community, with a budget of $18 billion. Clinton also appointed a new CIA chief, James Woolsey. During his Senate confirmation hearings, Woolsey remarked that "in some ways, the hottest current topic in intelligence policy. . . . The very difficult question on this (is) whether the U.S. government under any circumstances should share any types of economic intelligence with private citizens or corporations."[8] To learn more about the issue, Woolsey prepared a report along with National Security Advisor Anthony Lake and one of the chief White House economists, Robert Rubin.

At the time of his departure, and as a result of his resignation on December 29, 1994, because of the Ames fiasco, CIA Director Woolsey had already explained a few aspects of the CIA's new focus: "We are not in the business of spying for private firms. But it does mean that we bring these corrupt foreign practices to the attention of the White House and the state and commerce departments, who then seek redress—often successfully."[9] Naturally, to fight effectively against a company or a country playing dirty in the commercial realm, one needs information about major players and their doings—production, research, cash flow, sales networks, middlemen. And all of this looks a whole lot like old-fashioned espionage. Woolsey's new line wasn't ignored, for wasn't he saying just what many wanted to hear? As a CIA operative said to the *Wall Street Journal:* "There's historical animosity between government and business, and many executives don't want to be tainted by association with spies. Perhaps that's why ATT says 'We don't need the CIA's help in these kinds of matters, thank you very much.'"[10]

The big change was announced officially by Bill Clinton on July 14, 1995. Before an audience of CIA officials at their headquarters in Langley, Virginia, the president clearly reaffirmed his intention not to dismantle the agency, since he didn't believe in, "cancelling your health insurance when you're feeling fine."[11] While admitting that the Cold War was over, he stressed that the new stakes were economic and that the United States was ready for them: "A few have urged us to scrap the central intelligence service. I think these views are profoundly wrong. . . . Our nation is at peace, our economy is growing all right. All around the world, democracy and free markets are on the march. But none of these developments are inevitable or irreversible and every single study of human psychology or the human spirit, every single religious tract tells us that there will be troubles, wars and rumors of war until the end of time."[12]

The president went on to discuss the active roll the CIA plays in economic and industrial espionage, offering frank pronouncements on the importance of such initiatives. Clinton did stress that these governmental efforts were only used to help honest American companies combat dishonest competitors whose tactics are getting in the way of American successes. Clinton warmly praised those who helped "uncover bribes that would have cheated American companies out of billions of dollars. . . . Your work has promoted American prosperity."[13]

Los Angeles Times reporter James Risen explained the degree to which the American information services are mobilizing around this new battleground, allowing White House economists "to be pleased with the CIA's success at adapting to its new industrial and economic missions. An internal debate about the proper role for the CIA in economic espionage has led officials to conclude that such counterintelligence activity is one area where the agency can and should play a role. CIA officials believe that they should not conduct espionage directly against foreign firms on behalf of U.S. corporations and should limit their covert economic espionage to such areas as trade negotiations, protection of American firms against penetrations by foreign intelligence agents and uncovering bribes and corruption involving foreign businesses or officials that make it difficult for U.S. firms to compete in developing countries and elsewhere."[14]

In fact, the CIA's success in this domain has not been limited to merely assisting Raytheon in Brazil. It is accepted and admitted in private by American information professionals that government information espionage efforts have been put at the disposal of many U.S. firms, particularly the automobile industry. "But the thieves won't be a neighborhood gang, nor will they be part of an organized crime ring. You will have papers to prove that you bought the car, and every month you will make payments to a bank. The bank, in turn, will show that it bought title from Ford, General Motors, or Chrysler. But the Big Three U.S. auto companies will nonetheless be the recipients of stolen goods. And the perpetrator once again will be that expert at black-bag jobs, the Central Intelligence Agency."[15] It has been reported that during tense negotiations with the Japanese over automobile imports and exports in early 1995, the American negotiators were being fed information by secret American agents. But this wasn't the only time that Mickey Kantor, chief negotiator of that period, benefited from big-name help.

During the GATT (General Agreement on Tariffs and Trade) negotiations between the United States and Europe in 1993 and 1994, France was taking such a hard line that the NSA took a hard look at the French government. Since French cabinet ministers have the convenient (or annoying, depending on your point of view) habit of calling their offices from the air, their conversations during the most sensitive final period of the negotiations were vulnerable to interception: no encryption system protects them. This sort of thing is child's play for the NSA. A similar lack of sense was displayed during negotiations in Saudi Arabia: then French prime minister Édouard Balladur broadcast the Europeans' final move across the defenseless airways, helping Airbus Industries lose out to Boeing and McDonnell Douglas. One might argue that the contract was already as good as lost given the political pressure the United States had been adding to the proceedings, Bill Clinton personally intervening on several occasions in talks with Saudi Arabia's King Fahd.

Communications espionage is not monopolized by the United States. The French and their DGSE are also adept at this useful art and received no small satisfaction in intercepting the phone calls of Paul Kagamé, the Tutsi leader, after his conquest of Rwanda in 1994. This allowed French president François Mitterrand to launch Operation Turquoise, the French initiative in Rwanda under the aegis of the U.N. in summer, 1994. The rebel leader had been given a gift by the United States: a portable satellite telephone hooked up to *Inmarsat*, which proved perfectly transparent to the French. As soon as the

United States figured out that Kagamé's communications were being intercepted, he was quickly provided with better equipment.[16]

An American in Paris (the CIA, That Is)

In early 1995, with tensions running high between France and the United States due to competition over international contracts, France's minister of the interior, Charles Pasqua, led a move to expel a group of CIA spies from France.[17] There were clear political motivations behind the effort, serving to further the campaign of Édouard Balladur in his bid for the presidency. However, what makes the incident stand out is the degree to which the blunders of the CIA spies were talked about in the press. Officially, friendly nations aren't supposed to spy on each other on the other's home soil; what made this case so unusual wasn't that the CIA was spying on the French on their soil but that the CIA got caught! Furthermore, in situations similar to this that have occurred between allies in the past, it has been very rare for this sort of laundry to be publicly aired.

It didn't hurt to have some major disputes as backdrops to the main event, many settled at the time by the DGSE's varied infiltrations of American companies (IBM, for example) during the 1980s. Of course, though Claude Silberzahn had smoothed things over pretty well with the United States in that debacle, the French had earned a reputation in the United States as cheats. It didn't help that one of the diplomats watched by the CIA in this period, Bernard Guillet, was moved from his post as French

consul general in Houston to the office of Minister
Charles Pasqua where, as diplomatic advisor to the
minister of the interior, he helped manage the whole
CIA business.[18]

During a period when the United States was ad-
justing it's ways of doing business in the world of intelligence by doing intelligence in the world of business, such moves were conspicuous and the stakes
high. The United States believed it was a matter of
life and death for many American firms. Eliminating
their competitors in the space, arms, telecommunications, and agricultural industries became a top
priority, whether the information that made such
initiatives came from the private or public sector.
The failure of the American agents in their attempt
at Parisian penetration—though none of the agents
were ever actually expelled—was seen as a disaster
in Washington. By order of the Senate, CIA inspector general Frederick P. Hitz led an investigation and
charges flew. One of John Deutch's first decisions
when he took over the CIA in May 1995 was to punish Joseph De Trani, the chief of the European division. He was forbidden from coming to Paris to re-
place Dick Holme, who had been head of the group
that botched the attempt at penetrating the French
government.[19]

Despite forward steps, companies are having
difficulty dealing with the challenges presented by
the gathering and analysis of information. One of
the leading specialists on this subject, Philippe Baumard, states the problem this way: "Organizations
lack time to understand their environment. Information flows in from everywhere, sinking the corporate ship under tons of urgent needs, the latest

special reports, a 24 hour a day accumulation of on-line news, and so on. . . . Companies can be seen as interpretation systems whose scanning, interpreting and learning are interrelated in a close and dualistic relationship. Scanning is at the core of the relationship between a company and its environment, and is thus a key to understanding corporations. A company does not function in an ocean of information, ready to be gathered and incubated within an explicit interpretation cycle."[20]

Many private information companies have blossomed to fill the need, using all the basic strategies and means of their secret service counterparts to address the concerns of the private sector, acting as subcontractors to the big businesses. Although little known to the wider world, the French company Inforama International is one of the world leaders in economic information gathering. Inforama International is a subsidiary of Inforama, a conglomerate founded by Robert Guillaumot, a former artillery officer and secret service specialist in high technology. Inforama has been growing rapidly throughout Asia and has a subsidiary in the United States called Hitech Consulting Group which devotes its attentions to developing software, telecommunications, and computer technology. Employing 225 engineers and managers, Inforama has capitalized on a synergy involving the development of software, on the one hand, and the setting up of information-gathering offices throughout the world, on the other. Their software is used by the French government and ranges from electronic war simulations to programs that interpret the images from spy planes and spy satellites. Their information-gathering offices are employed by

France's top companies, offering spectacular results that, not surprisingly, no one wants to talk about specifically. Discretion is their guiding light.

Professional Clubs and Open Sources

It comes as no surprise that Inforama's founder was interested enough in the Society of Competitive Intelligence Professionals (SCIP) to found a French branch. SCIP is a watering hole for independent economic information hunter-gatherers. A fraternity of the like-minded and like-employed, the club offers its members a relaxed atmosphere for the exchange of ideas. Founded in the United States in 1986 by Faye Brill and now led by Tracey Scott of Pacific Bell Information Service, SCIP has around three thousand members who gather each year for an annual conference to commiserate over the ideas of the Swedish economic infomatician Stevan Dedijer, whose writing vanguards the idea of "open information"; they discuss *Competitive Intelligence Review* and the ethical questions surrounding their work. In their view, competitive information—the gathering and analysis of information on a business's competitors—cannot be gathered except in a regulated environment. They state their creed on their Internet site: "To continually strive to increase respect and recognition for the profession. To pursue one's duties with zeal and diligence while maintaining the highest degree of professionalism and avoiding all unethical practices. To faithfully adhere to and abide by one's company policies, objectives and guidelines. To comply with all applicable laws. To accurately disclose all relevant information, including one's identity and organization, prior to all interviews. To fully respect all requests for confidentiality of information. To promote and encourage full compliance with these ethical standards within one's company, with third party contractors, and within the entire profession."[21]

The big difference between the state-run information services and the businesses doing economic infotration isn't only the size of their operations: they also go about their work using radically different methods. In theory (true in most situations), private companies balk at the idea of resorting to illegal means, which are the bread and butter of the secret services. The secret services operate on the edge of law and government, generally in an effort to thwart the actions of groups, individuals, or governments willing to use means prohibited by law and which the legal system has difficulty controlling. Of course, the secret services also take it upon themselves to collect economic information illegally via all means new and old.

The purview of private infotration enterprises remains the world of "open" information that allows, thanks in large part to the latest methods of enhanced information, to find large quantities of information in available literature, mostly via electronic means. Certain experts say that 95% of what they want is already available in this form[22]: the remaining 5% is what the governmental secret services are trying to get. Robert Steele, one of the world's leading experts on the subject, has been lobbying for entirely open sources. Steele, whose business is called Open Sources Solutions, believes that all sorts of problems would be solved by such an arrangement, as well as by recasting the complete American information-gathering apparatus around his concept of Open Sources Intelligence (OSCINT), which he presented to the CIA in a memorandum dated July 1993:[23] "I focused on the radical change in the threat spectrum that intelligence must deal with today. On the impact that OSCINT could have on both analysis and consumer satisfaction, and on the broader context within which intelligence could contibute to our national security and national competitiveness, as part of a larger national 'information continuum' which could be fully engaged to meet consumer needs. . . . At this defining moment in the history of US intelligence, needed are leaders of vision and character, willing to take risks, to open minds, and to move forward with the reinvention of US intelligence."[24]

Officially, Steele is seen as something of an iconoclast by the CIA, where he served as head of operations in South America before joining the Marine Corps to rebuild the Marine Corps Intelligence Center. Now having reintegrated into private enterprise, Steele is doing his best to convert those around him to his view of the world. Despite the CIA's on-again off-again relationship with him, Steele seems to be succeeding: the CIA recently created a position, manned by Paul F. Wallner, dedicated to the study of open sources. Wallner was present for the second plenary session of the OSS (Open Sources Solutions) in October 1993.

Steele has even been looking for disciples in France. Although he has had some success there, mostly in the DGSE and DRM, the minister of the interior is none too pleased. With Steele's background some find him a difficult man to trust despite his pronouncements about his previous employer, the CIA. In France the pursuit of this sort of "open information" is against the law.[25] Hence, when the OSS tried to hold a conference in Paris on the subjects of open sources and the information superhighway, the French authorities requested that they abandon the idea.

The Japanese, Masters of Infonomics

The specter of the Japanese looms large in the world of economic information gathering. According to most specialists on the subject, including François Jakobiak, director of the economic intelligence network at Atochem,[26] the Japanese achieve startling results because of their excellent techniques. Japan "has been concentrating on a meticulous, systematic combing through of the world's store of published information, particularly concerned with data on the major industrialized nations. This careful surveillance and prudent use of information has led to their stunning successes. If the major companies in the United States, France, Germany and Great Britain are having difficulty seeing the necessity of working together, and if some of their directors wish that they were getting a little more help from their governments, the same can't be said for the empire of the Rising Sun. If the Japanese have succeeded first by imitating us and then going on to create on their own, why shouldn't we, now, be the ones to imitate them?"[27]

In Japan there is little disagreement over this issue: information gathering for the benefit of private enterprise is the *sine qua non* of their success. The Naicho division of the prime minister's office is responsible for serving as liaison between the government information services and private enterprise. Christian Harbulot, one of France's experts on the ins and outs of the Japanese economy, says that the relationship between private managers and government information agencies is a privileged one: "Today, Japan's ability to gather information has become the world standard in speed and depth. Other countries' databases pale in comparison to those of the Japanese and show no sign of catching up in the foreseeable future. The Japanese are already in a position to bring the countries of the world to the negotiating table to offer them access to a worldwide information network that would be under Japanese control. By ensuring the flow of information and by strategically controlling its contents, Japan is in the process of changing the rules of economic war to suit its interests."[28]

Despite these leaps forward, the Japanese have not taken to the Internet or to data transfer networks in general. Japan has helped equip many Asian countries with high-speed data lines connected one way or another to their network analysis tools (search engines, etc.), and they do foresee a vast expansion of the information superhighway, including, within twenty years, fiber-optic connections in every house. Despite this actual and projected expansion, the Japanese have no interest in using these networks for personal communication. Haruhisa Ishida, a driving force behind the Internet in Japan, explains that the primary concern of those who work in the Ministry of Education is that they end up controlling the servers that link to the world networks. Haruhisha says that they have no interest even in trying to understand the Internet and why it's so popular: "Even when we explain it to them, they still don't understand."[29]

As Nicholas Negroponte, the driving force behind MIT's Media Lab and one of cyberspace's leading figures affirms, the Japanese are responsible for introducing a communications technology which has taken over the world: the fax machine. "Fax is a Japanese legacy, but not just because they were smart enough to standardize and manufacture them better than anybody else. It is because their culture, language, and business customs are very image-oriented. . . . The pictographic nature of kanji made the fax a natural. Since little Japanese was then in computer-readable form, there were few disadvantages. On the other hand, for a langage as symbolic as English, fax is nothing less than a disaster, as far as computer readability is concerned."[30]

Japan's reluctance to adapt to the information age has prompted experts like Kent E. Calder of Princeton University to start sounding like Cassandra as they berate the country for its apparent shortcomings: "In this new world, many of the old parochial practices and forms of organization that have long been exalted as Japanese strengths, including the country's venerable biases toward giant collective projects and indiscriminate bureaucratic intervention, tend to seem increasingly out of date. . . . Japan also remains notably slow for a technologically advanced nation to develop Internet

services. Indeed, the world's second largest economy currently possesses fewer than five percent of
global Internet hosts, compared to nearly two-thirds
of the global total for the US. . . . Now is the time for
Japan to think seriously, in cooperation with the
world community, about how to make itself more at-
tractive as an international business center. Change
is crucial to avoid the 'bypass phenomenon' that
threatens to condemn Japan, despite its massive
economic scale and industrious people, to increasing competitive irrelevance in the information
age."[31] By all accounts it seems that the Japanese
are neither deaf to these assertions nor unable to respond to them quickly. Aversion to the Internet en-
dured as late as 1995, but seems to have dissipated
spectacularly, replaced by rampant enthusiasm. Internet promotors took a didactic route, educating
the masses on the positive role that networks can
play in everyday life: "Traditionally, the Japanese
have regarded the government and bureaucracy as
the 'above,' designating them the task of public safety and welfare, and tended to complain when things
did not go as well as they wished. However, the 'public' must be maintained by the 'private' creating their
own set of rules, which is called self-rule. If they in-
dulge in such a designation of tasks to the officials,
without doing on their own initiative, they would end
up choking themselves."[32] In 1996 the Internet exploded in popularity throughout Japan. Once far behind the United States and Scandinavia, Japan has
been making up for lost time with huge leaps forward. In June 1996, Data Corporation published its
first Information Imperative Index, which rates a
country's (that is, its citizens) ability to take part in

the information society. Countries are classed from least to greatest as "joggers" (China, Turkey, Saudi Arabia), "sprinters" (Russia, Chili, Ireland), "striders" (England, Canada, Australia, Israel, Japan), or "roller bladers" (United States, Sweden). The striders are characterized by "purposeful, successful long-term internet investments marked by caution, conviction and consistency." In fact, Japan is moving at the speed of light. The telecommunications giant, Nippon Telegraph and Telephone (NTT), has launched the Open Computer Network (OCN) with which they hope to connect the majority of Japanese netsurfers. During 1996, Japanese Internet subcriptions rose from 1.5 million to 8.5 million, truly explosive growth.[33]

The former apparent Japanese distaste for the Internet has nothing to do, apparently, with a disinterest in the march of progress. On the contrary, the Japanese are driven by the idea of technological advancement, and businesses are using the networks for information and surveillance with the same expertise as their American and European counterparts, some with the same interest in using the Internet as a pathway for infiltrating distant databases. The Japanese prime minister has his own embryonic intelligence service called the Japan Information Center of Science and Technology, and the most important such organization in Japan is called the Japan External Trade Organization (JETRO), considered the equal of any of the information services in the developed world. There are eighty JETRO branches throughout the world, each charged with gathering all available information and hunting down anything conspicuously unavailable.

In the same way, although even more closely woven into the fabric of the various economies that they target, the famed organizations known as *sogo sochas* employ over sixty thousand employees globally and gather up everything they can find. Hundreds of these operatives circulate in every major city (over a thousand each in Paris, New York, and Washington, D.C.), taking part in collective bodies or specific businesses (Nomura, Mitsubishi, Daiwa), working in all sectors imaginable, haunting the places where professionals gather, actually or virtually, and sending in daily reports to their headquarters in Japan. By virtue of this setup they are able to react to most market changes faster than anyone, anticipating changes in legislation and adapting their products to exceed old standards and set new ones while everyone else plays catch-up. They have learned to juggle European legislation better than anyone, and have ended up selling more cars, motorcycles, electronics, and household appliances than all their competitors.

The Internet pioneers of the early 1990s, various Japanese subsidiaries of American companies, managed to get Internet connections after tough negotiations with the Japanese government. The main network, IIJ (Internet Initiative Japan), remained for some time under house arrest, abandoning those who wanted access to slow, rudimentary, and transparent connections available through universities. Connections for the general public have only recently been made available by companies like Bekkoame, which has been providing service since September 1994. But a decision by the Economic Planning Agency[34] to launch a Web about the Japanese economy seemed more an event for the local press than evidence of the dawning of a new era: "The Internet has revived the struggle for power. [. . .] This crisis, which reveals the limits of technological enthusiasm in Japan, also demonstrates that the country is incapable of understanding the fundaments of modern politics, notably the principle by which a country's citizens are the foundation of democracy."[35]

Well before the Internet tsunami engulfed Japan, many businesses had already designed and put in practice strategies suitable to an information society, strategies addressing the needs of professional users and buyers of information: they have every intention of using the network and have a long-term strategy in mind. Soon, following the example of Comline News Service,[36] a huge database of online information wil be made available, for a price. The database will be linked, among others, to Dialine-II at the Mitsubishi Research Institute and will offer technical and commercial information: "In order to become the primary source of scientific and technical information in the world, the Japanese first developed their information, carefully filtering and measuring it out for translation into foreign languages, using the language barrier to their advantage. Now they can move to the stage of super-information, selling the tested and finished products of their information industry. By giving economic intelligence a more prominent position within their industries, Japanese employers are integrating the collective information culture and the real-time management of data with the formulation of corporate strategies."[37]

They can do it, too. Of the more than three thousand databases throughout Japan covering every conceivable interest, only 353 were accessible from outside the country by the end of 1994. Recent statistics provided by the Database Promotion Center of Japan show that the most frequently consulted databases are: JOIS-JICST, scientific literature; PATOLISJAPIO, certificates, licenses, diplomas; COSCOS2 (TeikokuDtanank), companies and business; TSR-BIGS, financial data; TKC, legislation; KFC, fried chicken; and QUICK, stock markets. Clearly, the Japanese seem to be in an excellent position to dominate this new market. Displaying a somewhat suspect candor at their site on the World Wide Web, the Database Promotion Center's promotional director, Keisuke Okomuzi, says of their server: "The overseas need for Japanese information continues to increase. And Japan is now obliged to promote international distribution of Japanese information."[38]

10
High Stakes at High Noon

On February 4, 1994, a minor event of considerable symbolic importance took place. Bill Clinton exchanged e-mail with Swedish prime minister Karl Bildt who was thanking him for lifting the trade embargo against Vietnam that had been in effect since 1975. Bildt, making the most of the opportunity, wrote that it seemed appropriate that the United States and Sweden were the first to use the Internet as a means of diplomacy and communication. Clinton responded prophetically that he shared the prime minister's enthusiasm for the possibilities that this new technology promised. Only a year into his presidency, Clinton had already received over one hundred thousand e-mails in his personal electronic mailbox.[1] Nonetheless, very few diplomatic messages of any importance are sent via the Internet: it's just too unreliable, for the moment, to rise beyond symbolic status.

Do We or Don't We?

As a rule, "information war" is viewed as conflict between countries or companies, which, by definition, use many means to compete or fight in cyber-space. There are other battlegrounds as well, and the conflicts to come between the haves and the have-nots are already taking varied shapes around the world.

In the distant past, having a telephone, a car, a television, or indoor plumbing marked vast differences in social status between the haves and the have-nots. Now, going online is a status symbol. Nonetheless, monied or not, college-educated individuals as a group are rarely without a personal computer in the workplace or at home, at least half of which are connected to modems. It is almost inconceivable for college students not to use computers, their own or machines provided by the universities. It has become nearly impossible for scientists, academics, or business people to do their jobs without computers.

In 1994, Americans spent $8 billion on computer equipment, almost as much as is spent annually on new televisions. One figure speaks louder that the rest: 30% of American households have a computer. Not all of them are connected to online services, but the idea of the Internet is spreading and is being talked about and used further and further off the beaten track. The advantages to such a system are so clear that a sort of "cyberdemocracy" is in the air, which promises to allow average citizens to get in touch directly with politicians despite the impediments that overloaded, end-of-the-millennia schedules can create. E-mail doesn't interrupt a meeting and doesn't drown its recipients in the tons of paper as faxes would. Already, special interest groups send their petitions by e-mail, and members of Congress reach their constituents electronically. Commercial service providers such as GEnie, CompuServe, Prodigy, and America Online offer their customers specialized services that allow access to politicians who are all for this direct access: the link between the electorate and their offices is direct and practically free, allowing politicians to spend their time and money on things other than the television commercials upon which they used to be dependent. Some politicians even have their own servers, offering voters the opportunity to visit sites on a particular subject or pending issue or to read up-to-date position papers by their representatives on important issues of the day.

Pierre Lévy provides an optimistic view of this issue.[2] Lévy does not foresee a direct transfer of the current voting procedures to the virtual realm—no congressional or presidential elections by e-mail. When Lévy looks at the evolution underway, he is evaluating how network technologies will impact the emergence of a truly direct democracy. Lévy believes the existence of such a mechanism in cyberspace " . . . would allow everyone to help develop and refine shared problems on a continuous basis, introduce new questions, construct new arguments, and formulate independent positions on a wide range of topics. Together citizens would elaborate a diverse political landscape that was not preconstrained by the gaping molar separation among different parties. The political identity of the citizens would be defined by their contributions to the construction of a political landscape that was perpetually in flux and by their support for various problems (the most important), positions (to which they would adhere), and arguments (which they would in turn make use of). In this way everyone would have a completely individual identity and role, distinct from any other individual, coupled with the possibility of working with others having similar or complementary positions on a given subject, at a given moment. Obviously some means would be needed to protect the anonymity of political identities. We would no longer participate in political life as a 'mass,' by adding our weight to that of the party or by conferring increased legitimacy on a spokesperson but by creating diversity, animating collective thought, and contributing to the elaboration and resolution of shared problems."[3] Far from believing that this new technological tool will alienate the average citizen from new means of communication, one is inclined to agree with Lévy that the personal computer's complexities—much like those initially presented by television, the telephone, and the automobile to earlier eras—will be conquered and will become integral parts of our daily lives.

"Personal newspapers,"[4] constitute another service which their users will have to master. The *Charlotte Observer, USA Today,* the *Chicago Tribune,* the *Albuquerque Tribune,* and the *Saint-Louis Post-Dispatch* have all been online for some time. The *Wall Street Journal*[5] has its own server, and the *New York Times*[6] is available through America Online and the World Wide Web. The *Washington Post* is on the Web,[7] with a very good free interactive edition. The *Los Angeles Times* is also available on the Web,[8] and offers access to its archives at a cost of $1.50 per article. So many new newspapers and magazines are appearing each month on the Internet that those who do not have Web sites will soon be the exception. In Europe, London's *Daily Telegraph* is available in virtual form as the *Electronic Telegraph,* and soon papers in France and the rest of the continent will follow suit with electronic versions of their national papers. *Libération,*[9] one of the major French national papers, has its own Web site, and Globe Online offers its subscribers a variety of papers to choose from. The French daily newspaper *Le Monde* also has its own site,[10] and in 1996 thousands of other publications made their way onto the Web. *L'Hebdo,* a Swiss site out of Lausanne, has an excellent "display" of various world press sites, indispensible for those interested.[11] There has also been the emergence of newpapers that exist only online, as Pointcast and MSNBC, a joint venture by Microsoft and NBC Television.[12] This evolution toward the Internet, based on clear economic and editorial strategies, raises some serious questions.

How will people who don't know how to use computers be able to function in this increasingly technologically dependent society? How can one communicate electronically if one is illiterate? How can one gain the expertise necessary to master such means without spending the considerable sum necessary to buy a basic machine?

In the United States, the issue is being given considerable attention and was addressed by Commerce Secretary Ron Brown: "How do you create an environment so that once we've built this information infrastructure, you do not create a society of haves and have-nots?"[13] Already, among similarly skilled workers, those who are computer literate earn 15% more than their colleagues who are not. Within American school systems, a further schism between the haves and the have-nots is occurring. Some students learn in classrooms equipped with powerful computers and Internet connections and have teachers who can integrate the Internet and Websurfing into the educational process. In other schools, students are lucky if they all have textbooks: "To less fortunate students, the Information Highway is about as real as the yellow brick road to Oz."[14]

Far from heralding a new democratization of education, the Internet may drive a yet more powerful wedge between rich and poor, insiders and outsiders, the well-educated and the illiterate. Many people are leaning in the direction of this argument, prognosticating the presence of icebergs lurking below the waterline of history into which the Titanic Age of Information may be heading: "The progress being made in information technologies must be taken in equal measure with an awareness of their impact on society. Of particular concern should be the increase in scientific and technological illiteracy, a phenomenon which can only limit the benefits such technology could have, and can even set the stage for a domination of our democratic political system. New programs are needed to aid in the development of the intellectual faculties that will be able to assimilate the fundamental changes brought about by the evolution of information technologies."[15]

Civil War?

Will the war between rich and poor find its way to cyberspace? If the possibility is already very real in the so-called developed nations, it is only fair to assume that such dynamics will soon come to bear in the Third World. The phone systems in place in Niger, Guatemala, and Kampuchea, for example, are not as sophisticated or complete as those in Europe, the United States, or Japan. The globalization of communication networks is a distinctly subjective idea, given that so much of the globe can't yet be included. Certain countries (India or Indonesia, for instance) have attracted some computer subcontracting, for programming and data capture in bulk, sent along to silent partners via electronic networks. Much of the information capture at work in Indonesia is very rudimentary: copying large, long texts like phone books. But in India, where the educational level of their operators is much higher, very sophisticated information sorting and software development are available at great savings over similar costs in Europe and the United States (the average Indian operator earns only three thousand dollars per year).[16] But real progress isn't yet being made, only a new application of cheap labor to the high-tech domain, work that would be too expensive to carry out at home. "The development of telecommunications has exposed services with weak added value (like routine management activities and invoicing) to competition from poorer countries. When moving at breakneck speeds along the information superhighway, richer countries try to make their less fortunate competitors let go. . . ."

Paul Virilio, urbanist and philosopher, has spent his life working on the subject of speed, in strategy and in war. In his eyes, the "immediacy of exchange" of information via virtual means portends grim business to come, a potential source of new inequities, both political and social: "Today, tyranny is taking to the virtual forum. As much as this instantaneous ability for individuals to electronically exchange information is marvelous, there is a redoubtable side to all of this interactivity. I am an internationalist. My father was an immigrant and I'm not about to use nationalism as a shield. I agree with the idea of a world citizenry that could be able to respect both borders and cultural differences. But I am suspicious of the idea of a supreme moment of human togetherness, of a unification of the planet. As I see it, unification is necessarily tyrannical. And that tyranny is what cyberspace is heading for, not Virtual Reality headsets. There is much at risk and we must fight because such an evolution needn't be inevitable."[17]

The problem isn't necessarily as cut and dried as such points of view might make it seem. There can be a very positive side to this technology, even if truly global access to information networks is a distant reality in developing countries. First of all, there are networks in place to help them connect to the Internet with a minimum of trouble. Peacenet, a California organization, gives hundreds of activist groups around the world access to the Internet, aiding their varied fights for education and human rights. Peacenet is a part of the APC network (Association for Progressive Communication), which also includes Econet[18] (devoted to questions relating to the environment and offering a link to the British ecological network Greenet), Conflictnet[19] (a network centered around mediation issues), Labornet (devoted to social reform), and WomanNet (centered around feminist issues). Networks have been popping up everywhere: the Third World Network in

India (TWN), Pegasus in Australia, Laneta in Mexico, Sangonet in South Africa, and many more.

The Internet is even making it possible for isolated Russian towns, otherwise entirely cut off from the rest of the world, to be connected by Glasnet.[20] When Russian trade unionists Alexander Segal, Boris Kagarlitsky, and Vladimir Kondratov were stopped by police in October 1993, Glasnet got them out of jail. It all started when the main trade union headquarters in Moscow sent an e-mail to its members and friends around the world, giving them the phone number of the police station where its members were being held. From the United States, Japan, and Europe, calls avalanched, burying the police under a world of pressure: the captors cracked and let the men go.[21] The story comes to us fourth-hand, but nonetheless reinforces the idea that the Internet can do more than carry newspapers, nourish spies, or breed capitalism.

In Africa only a few universities are connected to the Internet, and they only use it to send and receive e-mail. South Africa, Egypt, Tunisia, and Zambia are all Internet functional. The electronic newspaper *Econews Africa*, published in Nairobi, Kenya, and connected to the Internet via a Uruguayan network (NGOnet, a network of nongovernmental organizations based in Montevideo) keeps up to date on the ups and downs of African websurfers: "African internauts are positive that changes at policy level that have prevented connectivity in the past are likely to take place due to ongoing efforts to enable most of Africa to get internet connectivity in the next 1–2 years. . . . Of course, those using the technology in Africa face endless problems—busy telephone lines, breakdowns of modems, disappeared messages, desperate shortages of systems operators to resolve technical difficulties who are overworked and under-paid."[22]

Paradoxically, one of the remedies to Africa's lack of telephone wiring may come from the new and extraordinary satellite telephone networks that various international consortiums are all preparing to put into place. A dozen different ventures are under way, all competing for a slice of the virtual pie, and all of which have an eye on replacing the existing cellular phone networks already in service. Their idea involves having little portable telephones that link directly to satellites without requiring ground-based relays. One could imagine that the cost of such systems could potentially be far less, with all hardware installed in space. Iridium is the most advanced of the systems. It will go into service in September 1998 and will require the launching of sixty-six satellites in low-earth orbits. The project, costing $5 billion, is led by Motorola, which owns a quarter of the shares. Other investors include Sprint, Raytheon, McDonnell–Douglas, Lockheed, STET (Italy), and Verbacom (Germany). The first of Iridium's satellites launched in May 1997 from Vandenberg, California. But another program making rapid strides is Globalstar. Globalstar is the baby of Loral and Qualcom and has rich uncles in Alcatel and France Telecom. This system will use forty-eight satellites and will cost $1.7 billion. In high-earth orbit, two ventures aim to create networks comprising "only" ten satellites: Odissey and Oco. And Bill Gates and Microsoft are planning a $9 billion project that aims to launch 840(!) geostationary low-earth orbit satellites—problematic for the cost and the obvious complexity such numbers guarantee. France jumped into the ring in March 1997 with Alcatel's $3.5 billion Skybridge project; it aims to have sixty geostationary satellites in orbit. All this competition is sure to give the consumer maximum value and guaranteed freedom from their phone jack, and even from their national phone company.

Latin America has caught up quickly in telephonic infrastructure through use of similar technology: rather than running lines and poles across the countryside, cellular phones are being used. At the time of the G7 summit in February 1995 in Brussels, Belgium, Craig McCaw, one of the Teledesic partners, promised to offer access to his network, at cost, to users in developing nations. In China, which only has approximately twenty thousand phone lines, potential investors in the incredible communications market that awaits are getting dizzy from their profit projections. The market has been sized at $100 billion over the next ten years and will allow China to move straight from telephonic prehistory to high-speed data transfer, building a huge business out of new fiber-optic connections. Vietnam is just one step behind them.

The Last Crusade

Analysts estimate that the telecommunications market will explode to $1 trillion by the year 2000, up from $600 billion in 1993. This huge projected increase leaves little doubt that competition between public and private enterprise will intensify and that the three sectors of the market will be equally hard-fought.

The first part of this planetary cake involves the highway portion of the information superhighway. The biggest budgets will be earmarked for laying this infrastructure, which, whether concrete and steel or optical fibers, is always the big-ticket item. The European Commission estimates that it will cost $200 trillion to run high-capacity fiber-optic cable into the homes of all Europeans, twice the estimated cost of hooking up the United States. The U.S. federal government has no plans to pay for one cent of it: private enterprise will foot the bill. The cost of installing such an infrastructure in Asia is also projected at $100 billion, and one is forced to ask: who will build these networks? Telephone companies (whose copper wiring, however inadequately it may be suited to modern needs, is already everywhere) stand to try and preserve whatever monopolies they can, but the prospect of universal deregulation will allow cable companies and entertainment conglomerates to home in on this juicy new market, offering access to the Internet as well as telephone service and some form of interactive television. The need for all this new infrastructure in the form of wiring stems from a desire to send more information than the old wires can. If one wanted to send even one still photograph of broadcast quality over these copper wires, several minutes might be required to do the job. Cable companies, whose coaxial cables run into the television sets of millions of Americans, know that their preexisting cables can send the same still photograph of broadcast quality in a fraction of a second given the greater bandwidth (capacity) of the cables. Fiber optics offer the tantalizing possibility of even greater bandwidth than coaxial cable and, as many businesses hope, will allow downloading in real time of all sorts of media. These developments, however, have yet to take clear form.

The second tasty piece of the information market consists of the hardware into which these connections will lead. Various ideas and machine prototypes are already out there. The machines are projected to be multimedia-oriented (able to handle a variety of media) fusions of telephones, computers, and televisions, all digitally integrated and benefiting from huge memory on hard drives, CD-ROM, or as-yet-unimagined means. In the summer of 1996, Apple started selling its "Pippin" machine in Japan, the first dedicated Internet computer. There are surely more to follow.

Recently, several manufacturers introduced a new kind of hard drive which isn't a drive at all. PCMCIA (Personal Computer Memory Card International Association) cards are no bigger than credit cards and can hold up to a gigabyte of information, all for around five hundred dollars. They plug into the PCMCIA slots in many computers and have appealingly cutting edge product names like "Pocket Rocket." Currently, these cards are being snapped up by photojournalists whose memory-hungry digital cameras can download their payload of photographs into a convenient, lightweight package. While it is hard to say whether PC cards will be around for more than fifteen minutes of technological fame, the rapid development of smaller, more powerful means of storing information, coupled with the increased bandwidth that fiber optics will provide, should allow the Internet to channel all sorts of memory-heavy products into homes. Many media-smart people have thought of one potential application: selecting a film for viewing off the Internet that could be downloaded in real time directly into one's home. The proponents of this possible future imagine all the functionality of a VCR (pause, fast-forward, reverse) but many new features as well, such as choosing between original, dubbed, and subtitled versions of a film, in any language one could name. These techno-optimists envision cultural and educational products and interactive games. The potential revenues that could be produced in this futuristic market are colossal.

The third piece involves the information providers: this is where, if Europe plays its cards right, it can make major market inroads in database development, online sales, and much, much more.

But this three-layer cake will first have to be swallowed by consumers who could get a serious case of financial indigestion. These potential buyers represent the shaky foundation upon which this cyberstructure is being built. Even if the current Internet aficionados are paying relatively modest prices for their services, who is to say what the cost of connection will be in the future, and how much consumers will be willing to pay. In Europe the cost of telephone calls is far higher than it is in America. In Manhattan a one-hour local call from one's home to a friend's across town costs thirteen cents: in Paris, the cost is three dollars. Entrepreneurs in this domain no doubt feel little compunction about manipulating the habits of consumers, helping them empty their pockets into the coffers of investors.

One thing is certain: no one is playing it safe. The money on the tables of this new multimedia Las Vegas is piling up to the skies. Very quickly, the information industry is becoming the leading producer in the industrialized world. One insane example: Bill Gates and Craig McCaw, leaders in cellular telephone technology, have launched a venture which would be completely nuts had any one else tried it. The company that they started, Teledesic, has start-up capital in excess of $9 billion with which, before the year 2001, they plan to have launched 840 miniature satellites, the backbone for a global network of digital voice and data communications. Soon enough, those with telephones will only have one portable number that will follow them wherever they go, anywhere in the world: an oil refinery in Venezuela; the summit of Kilimanjaro; fishing for shrimp off the Louisiana coast. These communications will be of perfect technical quality, and subscribers will be able to send voice or computer data through the same handsets. The competition between Teledesic and Iridium will be fierce. But out of these battles, the consumer will be freed from in-house wiring and, in Europe and many other countries, governmental control of phone service.

The amount of money to be made in this new world is staggering. Start-up companies—those that have one big original idea and one big product—are capitalizing like never before in this "what's next is best" marketplace. Many of the companies that will go down in the history of 1995 were Internet-related software ventures, attempting to capitalize on the new market by making Internet access easier, quicker and more trouble free, with clear and practical graphic interfaces and search engines so user friendly that the most reluctant beginner is put immediately at ease. In 1995 alone, venture capitalists invested over $200 million in these companies, five times more capital than the previous year. Around this new information society, the future of the global economy is being built. The information wars that are brewing and flourishing under the flag of this new domain are sure to wreak havoc upon those who are left by the side of the road. Wall Street is ready to pounce on any opportunities in this new era and is spending its money on technology issues more than ever before. Netscape, the excellent Internet browser introduced in 1994, was initially distributed free of charge by Jim Clark on the Internet. Within six months, five million copies were downloaded. Clark then had Marc Andreessen, the program's creator, and Andreessen's team of programmers under contract at the time, improve the software. A better version was introduced, but this time it wasn't free. Few people who had used the program before decided to do without it. It sold. For service providers that had been using the counterpart to Netscape, Netsite, their ante was considerably higher: anywhere between six thousand and twenty thousand dollars. And to deal the final blow to Internet fanatics, Jim Clark made a public offering of Netscape on the New York Stock Exchange, August 9, 1995. Investors threw themselves at the stock and bought $2.13 billion worth. Only sixteen months since its introduction, Clark had managed to turn his initial $4 million investment into a real fortune.

With his perennial smartest-kid-in-the-class air and personal fortune in excess of $10 billion (making him one of the richest men, barring a few monarchs), Bill Gates sees himself killing off all his competitors in cyberspace. The tool by which he expects to leverage the market is no secret: Microsoft, the company he started with his friend Paul Allen, the most powerful software company in the world. With Windows 95, launched in August 1995, Gates tried to take hold of the Internet market with two star products: a proprietary network called, of all things, the Microsoft Network, and a navigator designed as a competitor to Netscape, Microsoft Explorer. In December 1995, the president of the Seattle company refocused his strategy. With business booming, his twenty thousand employeees and his $6 billion in sales he set his sights on a prime target; the Internet would be his new frontier, and Netscape wouldn't be the only flag in the soil. Microsoft Network was forgotten. In August 1996, after having put all his effort into this new focus, Gates unveiled his latest war machine: Microsoft Explorer 3, free, ready to compete with its rival. There were one million downloads in the first week. Since then, business as usual, with Gates putting Microsoft at the pole position. Explorer 4 has come out and Netscape is in a long, difficult race with a marathoner who also knows how to sprint across the United States and the rest of the world.

Epilogue

The war is under way. Forces bearing arms from computerized arsenals are advancing over the existing networks. So far, they're an elite bunch: Mr. and Mrs. America don't yet have fiber-optic connections in their rumpus rooms, kitchens, and dens. It will be a few years before they can get their hands on the heavy artillery. But they will: Al Gore wants us all to set out on the information superhighway, armed and ready, Mad Maxes of the megabytes, marching to information infinity and beyond.[1]

Among the many extraordinary aspects of this revolution is the relative accessibility of the technology. If you want to start a business peddling information, you can build your mousetrap in your garage and have the whole World Wide Web beat a path to it, to your Web site that is. And it will all be there—pictures of your vacation to Hawaii; the sound of birds singing in a garden; mathematical equations or musical compositions; underwear catalogs; the complete works of Chaucer in old English; dispatches from press agencies and military bulletins—everything and more will be available. Much of it already is.

Information war has already begun. Machines help humankind to communicate, to be understood, to learn, to perhaps promote a new kind of planetary democracy. But adherents of the old world order aren't happy about any of it and are doing everything they can to turn things around to the rules of the game they played in youth. The playing field, however, has changed forever, and the rules themselves no longer apply. Pierre Lévy reminds us: "In general, power has little affinity with the way the world works in real time. . . . Power tries to perpetuate advantages, to preserve acquisitions, to maintain situations, to block channels—dangerous goals during a period of rapid, large-scale deterritorialization."[2]

Unquestionably, barbaric conflicts are still tearing apart cultures, lands, and people; whether Stone Age or Information Age there seems no promise of an abatement. But in other parts of the world, war is changing and has found new battlefields. The armies of the world's democracies are becoming clumsy housekeepers, struggling to maintain a faltering *status quo*.

Information is the name of the game: buying, selling, watching, playing, and learning; there's plenty to spread around (true and false); there are fortunes to made and to be stolen. We still don't really know just where the information superhighway will lead when all is said and done, when all the road is laid. But already, in all walks of life, new rules are in play. The happy visionaries who pioneered the Internet and who wanted it to be a playground for the world, a generous and free utopia, don't want their baby to devolve into a capitalistic feeding frenzy: they want it to remain true to its beginnings. They want it to remain a place of communication and free exchange, without fear of snoops and with the understanding that this is a community of like-minded souls, not just another excuse for content providers, developers, and volume dealers.

But of course, this isn't how the secret services see the issue at all. They want to use the Internet to wedge their way into our private lives. They justify this intrusiveness with the cry that they will now be able to stop major crimes before they occur. They believe that in the name of national security they should have the right to look anywhere, anytime, despite the potential infringements on individual liberties that such initiatives imply. The new networks are already incredible means of investigation; if the secret services manage to obtain, despite outcry from the cybercommunity, the right and the means to read all electronic communications like open books and manage to prohibit the use of cyphers that they can't crack, the foundations of democracy will surely start to quake.

For the military, pioneers of armored communication, the logic of the networks has already been absorbed without incident. These tools that have given so many the ability to further democracy and interaction with our fellow human beings are perceived by the military as weapons of war ideal for the new struggle for information supremacy. At least they're right about that. Hackers can do some serious damage, and though someone better be ready for them, the Internet learns from these attacks. What remains to be seen is how the military will adapt use of the Internet to offensive strikes and in what circumstances such battles would be waged.

The United States is witnessing a head-on colli-
sion between those who would preserve our rights
wholesale across the electronic globe and those of
the new cyberorder who would seek certain conces-
sions in the name of what they claim as progress.
But with the speed at which the network is developing, these conflicts will soon spread everywhere that
the Internet extends. A major contradiction is in the
works, the Internet quickly becoming paradoxical:
at once apotheosis of democratic exchange and par-
adigm for the systematic suppression of individual
liberties. In Japan the philosophy of the network
flies in the face of traditions of societal control by the
government that are still in effect and which block
the successful proliferation of the network. In this
way Japan may be better protected from the potential downsides of global intercommunication, much
in the way that some companies keep clean by for-
bidding their employees from logging on: abstinence
remains the safest alternative. But can one really resist this movement? Nicholas Negroponte doesn't
think so: "The agent of change will be the Internet,
both literally and as a model or metaphor. The Internet is interesting, not only a massive and perva-
sive global network, but also as an example of something that has evolved with no apparent designer in
charge, keeping its shape very much like the formation of a flock of ducks. Nobody is the boss, and all
the pieces are so far scaling admirably."[3]

Is it giving the Internet too much credit to view
it as an agent of change? Time will tell. What is most
important right now is for those who are already
connected and those who will soon join them to
know what's at stake. Even in its current, rudimen-

tary incarnation, it's clear that the Internet is having an impact on our daily lives and society as we know it. Websurfers have adapted themselves to live in a world where distances don't exist and brick walls can be turned into paper partitions with a keystroke. These changes will only grow more pronounced; personal freedoms and democracy will be tested and will emerge stronger than before. But the battle is far from won.

Notes

Some Background on the Internet

[1] ARPA's mission statement then was the same as it is today, ". . . to develop imaginative, innovative and often high risk research ideas offering a significant technological impact that will go well beyond the normal evolutionary developmental approaches; and, to pursue these ideas from the demonstration of technical feasibility through the development of prototype systems." (Internet site: http://www.arpa.mil)

[2] Katie Hafner and Matthew Lyon, *Where Wizards Stay up Late: The Origins of the Internet*, Simon and Schuster, New York, 1996, pp. 10, 54–55.

[3] Most addresses consist of the last name of the user, followed by @ (pronounced "at"), and then the name of the service or company that provides the user with a connection to the Internet. The final part of the address is called the domain. It indicates the type of larger category to which the user would belong. If one were a student or a professor at a university, one's address would be followed by "edu"; a commercial user would have an address ending in "com"; military users, "mil"; government users, "gov," and so forth. In France, user addresses end in "fr," whereas in Great Britain they end in "uk," in Finland "fi," in Russia "ru," and so on. Yet, despite its organizational assistance, The Internet Society has no legal claim to the network, nor does it serve as administrator to the virtual entity. The Internet Society (Internet site: http://www.isoc.org/) is an extraordinary example of Internet self-management. ISOC was created in 1992 with the primary goal of guaranteeing fair compatibility for communications within the

263

cybercommunity. It has made no attempts to reign in the positive anarchic aspects of the community. The Internet remains a world without administrative oversight, without owners or stock holders, without official rules of conduct (for how much longer, one wonders).

4 Centre européen de recherche nucléaire.

5 Berners-Lee left Geneva in 1994 to found the non-profit World Wide Web consortium (W3C), based at MIT in Cambridge, Massachusetts.

6 The pioneers of hypertext came up with the idea of planting words in the net's various screens that would look different from those around them: they would appear in a different color or would be underlined. If a word were of particular interest (olive, say, if you wanted more information on the gourmet olives a pasta sauce called for), you could simply select it with your mouse ("clicking on" in cyberspeak) and find yourself transported to another screen that would give all sorts of information about it. A hypertext word, therefore, would allow you to move beyond, over, and above the word of interest to more related information.

7 The basic unit of numerical information is the *bit*. Eight bits are needed to make up each letter of the alphabet. Until 1996 it was commonly held that an ordinary telephone line would transfer a maximum of 28,800 bits of information per second (bps), or 28.8 Kbps (Kilobits per second). Since 1996, with the introduction of ADSL (Asymmetrical Digital Subscriber Lines), the ordinary copper wire can carry up to 8 megabits of information per second. Apparently, copper wiring isn't going down without a fight.

8 On May 20, 1996, thirty of the world's biggest computer companies, including IBM, Sun, Netscape, Akai, Nokia, and Motorola confirmed their intention to rapidly develop and market machines of this type. These giants were persuaded that this new type of machine would give them a foot in the door of tens of millions of users, breaking down one of the last market barriers—price—to having a computer in every home.

Chapter 1

1 He has since been appointed Russian foreign minister.

2 Direction générale de la sécurité extérieur.

3 Centre administratif des Tourelles.

[4] Claude Silberzahn with Jean Guisnel, *Au coeur de secret, 1500 jours aux commandes de la DGSE 1989/1993*, Fayard, Paris, 1995, p. 258.

[5] After years of complete silence surrounding its activities, the NSA has made baby steps forward. Nonetheless, its official internet site isn't very interesting: http://www.nsa.gov:8080. While there, take a look at "Opendoor, the National Security Agency's declassification effort." The National Security Archive's web is much more interesting. The Archive is a research institute that is a part of George Washington University. Official documents that have been declassified are available there via the Freedom of Information Act at http://www.seas.gwu.edu/nsarchive/. The indispensable resource on the NSA remains James Bamford's *The Puzzle Palace*, Houghton Mifflin Company, New York, 1982.

[6] *Phrack*, Number 45, March 1994.

[7] Do read Gibson's *Neuromancer* (which came out in 1984 and was written on an old-fashioned typewriter). It is a novel of mythic proportions.

[8] William T. Warner, "International technology transfer and economic espionage," *International Journal of Intelligence and Counter-Intelligence*, Volume 7, Number 2, Summer 1994.

[9] An extensive summary of these events is provided by Peter Schweizer in *Friendly Spies*, The Atlantic Monthly Press, New York, 1993. The reader may also turn to the fascinating study of John J. Fialka, *War by Other Means: Economic Espionage in America*; W.W. Norton & Company, New York.

[10] William T. Warner, *op. cit.*

[11] The OECD, Organization for Economic Cooperation and Development, was created in 1960 and organizes cooperative efforts at economic development. Of its twenty-four members, five are non-European: United States, Canada, Japan, Australia, and New Zealand.

[12] FATF report, OECD, February 7, 1990, p. 7.

[13] Ann Davis, "Nations worry about a rise in on-line money-laundering," *The Wall Street Journal*, March 17, 1997.

Chapter 2

[1] John Perry Barlow, "A not terribly brief history of the Electronic Frontier Foundation," November 8, 1990 [available through USENET (comp.org.eff.news)].

[2] Joshua Quitnner, "The merry pranksters go to Washington," *Wired*, June 1994.

[3] Mitchell Kapor and John Perry Barlow, "Across the electronic frontier," July 10, 1990.

[4] Mike Godwin, "The Electronic Frontier Foundation and virtual communities," 1991.

[5] Nouveau scandale en Espagne: le roi Juan Carlos était sur écoutes" ("New scandal in Spain: King Juan Carlos was tapped"), *Le Monde*, June 15, 1995.

[6] For more on this subject, see: Dorothy E. Dennings and Miles Smid: "Key escrowing today," *IEEE Commun.*, *32*, No. 9, September 1994, pp. 58–68; also found on Dorothy Denning's excellent crypto web page: http://guru.cosc.georgetown.edu/denning/crypto/.

[7] www.pathfinder.com, at which can be found a weekly selection of articles from the magazine.

[8] John Perry Barlow, "Jackboots on the infobahn," *Wired*, April 1994.

[9] Brock N. Meeks, "The end of privacy," *Wired*, April 1994.

[10] Stewart A. Baker, "Don't worry, be happy; why Clipper is good for you," *Wired*, June 1994.

[11] *Ibid*.

[12] "Information security and privacy in network environments," Office of Technology Assessment, Washington DC, September 1994.

[13] For a longer look at this incident, see Jonathan Wallace and Mark Mangan, *Sex, Laws and Cyberspace, Freedom and Censorphip on the Frontiers of the Online Revolution*, Henry Holt and Company, New York, 1996, pp. 1–40.

[14] Center for Democracy and Technology, Policy Post, February 9, 1995.

[15] www.solidoak.com/index.htm

[16] www.netnanny.com/netnanny/

[17] www.surfwatch.com/

[18] www.cyberpatrol.com/

[19] http://cyberwerks.com/cyberwire/

[20] Declan McCullagh and Brock Meeks: "Jacking in from the 'Keys to the Kingdom' Port." www.eff.org/pub/Publications/Declan_McCullagh/cwd.keys.to.the.kingdom.0796.article

[21] www.spectacle.org/

[22] http://peacefire.org/

[23] From an editorial in the *San Jose Mercury News*, the daily

paper of Silicon Valley, April 6, 1995. Internet site: http://www.sjmercury.com/.

[24] These included the American Library Association, Inc.; America Online, Inc.; American Booksellers Association, Inc.; American Booksellers Foundation for Free Expression; American Society of Newspaper Editors; Apple Computer, Inc.; Association of American Publishers, Inc.; Association of Publishers, Editors, and Writers; Citizens Internet Empowerment Coalition; Commercial Internet eXchange; CompuServe Incorporated; Families Against Internet Censorship; Freedom to Read Foundation, Inc.; Health Sciences Libraries Consortium; HotWired Ventures LLC; Interactive Digital Software Association; Interactive Services Association; Magazine Publishers of America, Inc.; Microsoft Corporation; Microsoft Network; National Press Photographers Association; NETCOM On-Line Communication Services, Inc.; Newspaper Association of America; Opnet, Inc.; Prodigy Services Company; Wired Ventures, Ltd.; and the Society of Professional Journalists Ltd.

[25] Mike Godwin, "Sinking the CDA," *Internet World*, October 1996.

[26] Cited by Godwin, *ibid.*

[27] Godwin, *ibid.*

[28] Judge Dalzell, *ACLU vs. Reno.*

[29] Statement by the president, June 12, 1996.

[30] Department of Justice Brief filed with the Supreme Court on January 21, 1997, available at site: www.cdt.org/ciec/.

[31] Enough is Enough, Childhelp USA, Citizens for Family Friendly Libraries, Computer Power Corporation, D/TEX Investigative Consulting, Focus on the Family, Help Us Regain the Children (H.U.R.T.), JuriNet, Inc., Kidz Online, Laura Lederer, J.D., Log-on Data Corporation, Legal Pad Enterprises, Inc., Mothers Against Sexual Abuse, National Association of Evangelicals, National Coalition for the Protection of Children and Families, National Council of Catholic Women, National Political Congress of Black Women, Omaha for Decency, One Voice/The American Coalition for Abuse Awareness, Oklahomans for Children and Families, Religious Alliance Against Pornography, The Salvation Army, Victims' Assistance Legal Organization, Weitzman, Lenore, Ph.D., Wheel Group Corporation.

[32] "A Framework for Global Electronic Commerce" is available at the site: www.iitf.nist.gov/eleccomm/ecomm.htm.

Chapter 3

[1] There is an excellent, comprehensive bibliography concerning Enigma available on the Internet: http://members.gnn.com/nbrass/biblio.htm.

[2] In reality, there is still some difference of opinion over the true paternity of the first computer, as some consider that a true computer must be programmable, something these early calculators were not. Those who defend Turing's pioneering role assert that, as of 1936, he conceived of programming, describing the principles in his university thesis (for more on this, see J. David Bolder, *Turing's Man, Western Culture in the Computer Age*, University of North Carolina Press, Chapel Hill, 1984, p. 12). Much has been written on this subject, but two of the best are David Kahn, *Seizing the Engma: The Race to Break the German U-Boot [sic?, Ed.] Codes, 1939–1943*, Houghton Mifflin Company, New York, 1991, and F.H. Hinsley and Alan Stripp, *Code Breakers, the Inside Story of Bletchey Park*, Oxford University Press, London, 1993.

[3] Von Neumann also envisioned recording programs in the memory of computers to come.

[4] Max Neuman, eminent professor of mathematics at the University of Manchester, who had worked with Turing during the war, had been one of·the first to recognize, as of 1936, the importance of Turing's research.

[5] Information on the dawn of computers was found in the writings of Philippe Breton, who teaches anthropology and contemporary sciences at the University of Paris I-Sorbonne: *Histoire de l'informatique*, Points-Seuil, Paris, 1990 and "Le premier ordinateur copiait le cerveau humain," *La Recherche*, Number 290, September 1996.

[6] During the early seventies, much information about the machine (also known as Ultra) was kept confidential by the British so that the Western powers could read the diplomatic communications of certain Third-World countries still using it.

[7] Those interested in learning more about cryptology will find an excellent FAQ (Frequently Asked Questions) about cryptology posted every 21 days in the following newsgroups: sci.crypt, talk.politics.crypto, sci.answers, and news.answers. The authors are Erich Bach, Steve Belovin, Dan Bernstein,

Nelson Bolyard, Carl Ellison, Jim Gillogly, Mike Gleason, Doug Gwyn, Luke O'Connor, Tony Patti, and William Seltzer. I used the version of January 11, 1994. Paul Fahn, an employee of RSA Laboratories, has also published a very well documented FAQ. I used version 3, summer 1995.

[8] Think of a key as a combination lock on a cheap suitcase or briefcase—indivual rollers marked with the digits 0–9 that will, when we have selected our combination—999, say—open the bag. For a computer to represent one of these digits and for it to distinguish a single digit (2) from any another (3), the computer needs eight pieces of typographical information about that digit, also called a "typographical sign." If we understand that we need eight *bits* of information to represent a single digit or typographical sign (these eight bits of information representing a typographical sign are called, collectively, a *byte*), then a sixteen digit number of code would be translated into sixteen bytes or 128 bits. Reasoning inversely, a computer key of 128 bits must be a number consisting of sixteen digits ($128 \div 8 = 16$). Thus, were we to buy a cheap suitcase lock with sixteen different rollers (rather than the customary three), this would still be far less complex than the same sixteen digits made into a computer key, which translates the sixteen digits into 128 bits of descriptive information.

[9] Jeff Lisquia, "Frequently asked questions on PGP," version of February 22, 1995. Available at alt.security.pgp, *or* http://www.praoroenet.org/~jalicqui/pgpfaq.txt.

[10] Many thanks to Serge Vaudenay of Groupe d'études et recherche en complexité et cryptographie for having shown me a thing or two about this stuff.

[11] Asymmetrical cryptography is another name for public key cryptography. As we explained it, it's a cryptography based on algorithms that enable the use of one key (a public key) to encrypt a message and a second, different but mathematically related, key (a private key) to decrypt the message.

[12] Bruce Schneier has written the very interesting and straightforward *Applied Cryptography: Protocols, Algorithms, and Source Code in C*, John Willey and Sons, New York, 1994.

[13] Phil Zimmerman, *PGP User's Guide*, PGP Version 2.3, June 13, 1993.

[14] Foreword by Philip Zimmermann, for *Protect Your Privacy: The*

PGP User's Guide, by William Stallings, National Computer Security Association, 1995.

[15] Scott Wooley, "Banned in Washington," *Forbes,* April 1997.

[16] Dorothy Denning, "To Tap or Not to Tap," *Comm. ACM,* March 1993, p. 33.

[17] John Perry Barlow, "Decrypting the puzzle palace," *Communications of the ACM,* Volume 35, Number 7, July 1992.

[18] *Ibid.*

[19] Steven Levy, "Crypto rebels," *Wired,* April 1993.

[20] From "Cypherpunks statement of purpose," by Eric Hughes, posted in the newsgroup sci.crypt, 1995.

[21] Steven Levy, "The encryption wars: is privacy good or bad?" *Newsweek,* April 24, 1995.

[22] Among a variety of Web sites, you can find the manifesto at http://swissnet.ai.mit.edu/6095/assorted-short-pieces/may-crypto-manifesto.html.

[23] Phil Dubois, Ken Bass, Eben Moglen, Curt Karnow, Tom Nolan, and Bob Corn-Revere.

[24] *San Jose Mercury News,* January 12, 1996.

[25] Including Jim Cowie, Marije Elkenbracht-Huizing, Wojtek Furmanski, Peter L. Montgomery, Damian Weber, and Joerg Zayer.

[26] For more on this subject, visit www.npac.syr.edu/factoring/status.html.

[27] Matt Blaze (AT&T Research), Whitfield Diffie (Sun Microsystems), Ronald L. Rivest (MIT Laboratory for Computer Science), Bruce Schneier (Counterpane Systems), Tsutomu Shimomura (San Diego Supercomputer Center), Eric Thompson (Access Data, Inc), and Michael Wiener (Bell Northern Research), "Minimal key lengths for symmetric ciphers to provide adequate commercial security," a report by an ad hoc group of cryptographers and computer scientists, January 1996.

[28] *Cryptography's Role in Securing the Information Society,* National Research Council, May 1996.

[29] Bruce W. McConnell and Edward J. Appel, "Enabling privacy, commerce, security and public safety in the global information infrastructure," Executive Office of the President, Office of Management and Budget, May 20, 1996.

[30] Janet Reno, "Law enforcement in cyberspace," address to the Commonwealth Club of California, June 14, 1996. Originally posted at http://pwp.usa.pipeline.com/~jya/adress.txt.

[31] Marc Rotenberg, "Testimony on the promotion of commerce on-line in the digital era (Pro-CODE)," before the Senate Committee on Commerce, Science, and Transportation, Subcommittee on Science, Space, and Technology, June 26, 1996.

[32] Administration statement on commercial encryption policy, July 12, 1996.

[33] Secrétariat générale de la défense nationale.

[34] Délégation interministérielle à la sécurité des systèmes d'information.

[35] Article 28 of Law 90–1170 of December 29, 1990, supplemented by Decree 92–1358 of December 28, 1992.

[36] E-mail address of the vice president: vice-president@whitehouse.gov.

[37] Apple Computer, Attala, Digital Equipment Corporation, Hewlett-Packard, IBM, NCR Corp., RSA, Sun Microsystems, Trusted Infortmation Systems, and UPS.

[38] CDT *Policy Post*, Volume 2, Number 35, October 3, 1996.

[39] "A flawed encryption policy," *New York Times*, October 4, 1996.

[40] "Crypto politics," *Washington Post*, October 4, 1996.

Chapter 4

[1] http://www.odci.gov/CIA/.

[2] BBS's, or Bulletin Board Systems, are information servers that serve the same function as Web sites. They are not, however, accessible through the Internet. They must be called directly on a special telephone number that is often unlisted. Only "members" (those with the phone number) can gain access to them and then collect information, download programs or leave them there for others, or exchange e-mail. Information hackers often use these systems to stockpile prohibited information (access codes, credit card numbers, "cracked" programs, etc.).

[3] Paul Wallich, "Wire pirates," *Scientific American*, April 1994.

[4] From a conversation with the author.

[5] For more on this topic, visit, among others, the newsgroups alt.2600, alt.hacking, and alt.cyberpunk.tech.

[6] Various interesting sites offering information on newsgroups include alt.security, comp.security.misc, misc.security, etc.

[7] To subscribe, send your email to LISTSER@VMD.CSO. UIUC.EDU.

[8] For more on the history of the LoD and on hacking in America, see Bruce Sterling's *The Hacker Crackdown: Law and Disorder on the Electronic Frontier*, Bantam Books, New York, 1992, which I consulted in preparing this information.

[9] Steven Levy, *Hackers, Heroes of the Computer Revolution*, Delta Books, New York, 1994, p. 40.

[10] Alternatively known as the Masters of Deceit or the Masters of Destruction.

[11] The telling of the tale is best done by Michelle Slatalla and Joshua Quittner in *Masters of Deception: The Gang That Ruled Cyberspace*, Harper Perennial, New York, 1995.

[12] Winn Schwartau, *Information Warfare: Chaos on the Electronic Superhighway*, Thunder's Mouth Press, New York, 1994, p. 204.

[13] Mark Abene (aka Phiber Optick), Julio Fernandez (Outlaw), John Lee (Corrupt), Elias Ladopoulos (Acid Phreak), and Paul Stira (Scorpion).

[14] Indictment, U.S. district court, southern district of New York, July 8, 1992. As quoted in *Information Warfare: Chaos on the Electronic Superhighway*, pp. 198–199.

[15] "Sentencing Puts Huge hacking Case to Rest," *San Jose Mercury News*, November 4, 1993.

[16] See Chapter 10.

[17] All correspondence may be addressed to letters@2600.com.

[18] This expression was used for the first time by Winn Schwartau on June 27, 1991, before the House Subcommittee on Technology and Competitiveness, Committee on Science, Space and Technology, U.S. House of Representatives.

[19] From a conversation with the author, September 1996.

[20] Firewalls are protection softwares designed to keep intruders out. Hackers love breaking through them by finding "backdoors" into the systems.

[21] Dynamic passwords change continuously and are managed by an autonomous system that monitors and aligns their constant evolution.

[22] *NCSA News*, April 1996.

[23] *Ibid.*

[24] For example, at the Internet site ftp://cdrom.com:/pub/security/coast/dict/wordlist.

[25] Internet site: www.promo.net/pg/.

[26] There are plenty of webs that are chock full of explanations of all manner of fraudulent entry and how to protect against it. Three among hundreds of resources: www.dc-sage.org/ security/security—hakkers.html, http://fireants. com/cnn/ cnn.shtml, www.onguard.on.com/onguard/index.htm.

[27] David Bank, "Satan's creator: a rebel for all seasons," *San Jose Mercury News,* April 5, 1995.

[28] Managed and largely written by Dan Farmer, COPS is a suite of shell scripts which forms an extensive security testing system; there's a rudimentary password cracker, and routines to check the filestore for suspicious changes in suited programs, others to check permissions of essential system and user files, and still more to see whether any system software behaves in a way which could cause problems. Alec Muffett (Alec.Muffett@UK.Sun.com). Posted in the newsgroup comp. security.misc, in 1996.

[29] *"Phrack* Magazine and Computer Security Technologies proudly present: The 1995 Summer Security Conference." Invitation posted to hackers newsgroups during spring 1995.

[30] *Ibid.*

[31] John Schwartz, "Chipping in to curb computer crime; federal authorities get high-tech help in tracking down hacker," *Washington Post,* February 19, 1995.

[32] Katie Haffner and John Markoff, *Cyberpunk, Outlaws and Hackers on the Computer Frontier,* New York, 1991. Last Edition, with a postface by Katie Haffner, Touchstone, New York, 1995.

[33] *Cyberpunk,* p. 349.

[34] Tsutomu Shimomura and John Markoff, *Takedown: The Pursuit and Capture of Kevin Mitnick, America's Most Wanted Computer Outlaw, by the Man Who Did It,* Hyperion, New York, 1996.

[35] *Takedown,* p. 313.

[36] Jonathan Littman, *The Fugitive Game, Online with Kevin Mitnick,* Little, Brown and Company, New York, 1996.

[37] Three Brazilian admirers of Mitnick have set up a Web site devoted to following the Mitnick trial: www.netmarket.com. br/mitnick/. See other web pages devoted to the Condor: www.well.com/user/littman/game/news.html; www.2600. com/kevin/; and his fan club's newsgroup: alt.fan.kevin-mitnick.

[38] Read Clifford Stoll's bestseller, *The Cuckoo's Egg,* Doubleday,

New York, 1989, in which he describes a trek across cyber-space in pursuit of a hacker who broke into his system and that led to the arrest in Germany of a fellow who had been furnishing the KGB with sensitive information for staggering sums of money.

39 A "beta version" of a software program is one nearly ready for general release. The programmer circulates this beta version among select users or friends to have them try it out and report any glitches or "bugs."

40 FTP servers that Internet Service Providers (ISPs) make available for use by their subscribers are for downloading freeware programs. Subscribers can also upload programs of their own making onto the server for others to later download.

Chapter 5

1 Direction de la surveillance de la territoire.

2 Interview with Jean-Bernard Condat, July 9, 1995.

3 The Godfrain Law provides that a long-distance computer break-in shall be punishable by imprisonment of up to one year, and a fine of up to $10,000. If the computer was damaged in the process, or data destroyed, the prison term may be increased to up to three years, and the fine to $100,000. If data was stolen for unlawful use, the prison term may be increased to up to five years, and the fine to $400,000. The actual text of the law is available at the site: www.cicrp. jussieu.fr/cicrp/loi-info.html.

4 E-mail address: anon@penet.fi. This protection is an illusion. In 1995, Finnish servers that allowed hackers to send files stolen from the Church of Scientology reported users' identities to the police. For more on this subject, see newsgroup alt.anon.

5 In 1995 the Finnish server (anon@penet.fi, one of the most famous on the Net) was sought by law enforcement officials for having taken in archives for storage that the Church of Scientology claimed had been stolen from them. The identities of the individuals who sent these archives were released to the police. For more on the use of the Internet by scientologists, read *Sex, Laws and Cyberspace, op. cit,* pp. 101–124.

6 For further information on the Helsingius affair, look at

Arnoud's website "Galactus" Engelfriet: www.stack.nl/~
galactus/remailers/index-penet.html].

[7] David Wise, *The Nightmover: How Aldrich Ames Sold the CIA to the KGB for $4.6 million*, HarperCollins, New York, 1995, p. 242.

[8] Peter Earley, *Confessions of a Spy: The Real Story of Aldrich Ames*, G.P. Putnam and Sons, New York, 1997, p. 317.

[9] Centre d'électronique de l'armement.

[10] Jean Guisnel, "Pirates en treillis," *Libération*, 12 mai 1995.

[11] After Michael Faraday, the noted physicist.

[12] Deborah Russel and G.T. Gangemi Sr., *Computer Security Basics*, O'Reilly and Associates, Sebastopol, CA, 1992, p. 253.

[13] Winn Schwartau, *Terminal Compromise*. You can read the book on Winn's website, undoubtedly the most interesting one devoted to information warfare and related matters: www.infowar.com].

[14] Robert Steele, *Theory and Practice of Intelligence in the Age of Information*, September 17, 1993.

Chapter 6

[1] The Unit for the Study of White-Collar Crime at the University of Liverpool has found that white collar criminals are responsible for most crimes involving embezzlement. *Intelligence Newsletter*, Number 210, February 4, 1993. Site: http://www.indigo-net.com/lmr.html.

[2] Club de la sécurité informatique français.

[3] Assemblée plénière des sociétés d'assurance-dommages.

[4] Cited by the Privacy Rights Clearinghouse (Center for Public Interest Law), San Diego, CA. http://cpsr.org/cpsr/factshts.

[5] One law passed by Congress in June 1986 was the ECPA (Electronic Communications Privacy Act). This and other laws and papers on the subject are available at the indispensable server of the House of Representatives: http://www.pls.com: 8001/his/12.html.

[6] Michael Meyer, "Keeping the cybercops out of cyberspace," *Newsweek*, March 14, 1994.

[7] Claude-Marie Vadrot and Louisette Gouverne, *Tous fichés*, First, Paris, 1994, p. 277.

[8] John Whalen, "You're not paranoid, they really are watching you," *Wired*, March 1995.

[9] Todd Lappin, "Truckin," *Wired*, January 1995.

[10] For more information on these difficulties, consult Henri-Pierre Penel, "Schengen, le fiasco informatique," *Science et Vie*, Number 935, August 1995.

[11] Guy Lacroix and Daniel Naulleau, "Maîtriser l'information," *Le Monde diplomatique*, mai 1994.

[12] Commission nationale informatique et libertés.

[13] CNIL, *Quinzième rapport d'activité 1994*, La documentation française, 1995, p. 268 *sq.*

[14] Groupe islamique armé.

[15] *Infomatin*, May 26, 1995.

[16] Mark Knobel, "Internet: nouvelle communication utilisée par les extremistes racistes et xenophobes?" in CNCDH, "Le reseau internet et les droits de l'homme," Paris, 1996.

[17] Union des étudiants juifs de France.

[18] Association française des professionels de l'Internet.

Chapter 7

[1] For more information on this subject, see Dominique Wolton, *War Game*, Flammarion, Paris, 1991.

[2] Garry H. Anthes, "Making US intelligence more intelligent," *Computerworld*, April 1991.

[3] Alan D. Campen, *The First Information War, the Story of Communications, Computers, and Intelligence Systems in the Persian Gulf War*, AFCEA International Press, Fairfax, VA, 1992.

[4] Lt Col. David Todd, "Gird for information war. US must control combat in cyberspace front," *Defense News*, March 6, 1995.

[5] As quoted by Craig L. Johnson, "Information warfare is not a paper war," *Journal of Electronic Defense*, August 1994.

[6] FM 100–6, released August 27, 1996, on the U.S. Army Web site: http://www.army.mil/.

[7] "Schools of history and imagination," *The Economist*, June 10, 1995. Also available on the Internet in an excellent file called "The Information advantage": http://www.earthlink.net./~the~economist/.

[8] Bruce Sterling, "War is virtual hell," *Wired*, Volume 1, Number 1.

[9] No definitive number has ever been published. Estimates run from 40,000 to over 200,000 dead. Three hundred and forty allied soldiers were killed.

[10] By the end of November 1995, the United States decided to launch Operation Train and Equip, at a cost of $400 million; in December 1996, this program had supplied Bosnian Muslims with 45 battle tanks, 80 infantry combat vehicles, 15 helicopters, and 46,000 assault weapons.

[11] Edward Luttwak, "Arm the Bosnians at last," *International Herald Tribune*, July 17, 1995.

[12] Alvin Toffler, *The Third Wave*, William Morrow and Company, New York, 1980. According to Toffler, primitive armies were a part of agrarian society (the first wave), and the great armies and machines of war were a part of the machine age (the second wave).

[13] Zaki Laïdi, *Un monde privé de sens*, Fayard, Paris, 1994, p. 143 sq. This theory has also been explored by Martin Shaw, *Post-Military Society*, Polity Press, Cambridge, 1991 and John Mueller, *Retreat from Doomsday. The Obsolescence of Major Wars*, Basic Books, New York, 1989.

[14] Jean-Louis DuFour and Maurice Vaise, *La Guerre au XXᵉ siècle*, Hachette, Paris, 1993.

[15] Alvin and Heidi Toffler, *War and Anti-war. Survival at the Dawn of the 21st Century*, Little, Brown and Company, New York, 1993, p. 249.

[16] Milnet (military Network) was initially a part of ARPANET. The two networks were separated in 1984, and ARPANET is now devoted solely to research.

[17] Defense Link: www.dtic.dla.mil/defenselink/
US Army: www.army.mil/
US Navy: www.navy.mil/
US Air force: www.af.mil/
US Marine corps: www.usmc.mil/
An impressive list of resources concerning the American army has been made up by the Canadian armed forces: www.cfcsc.dnd.ca/links/milorg/usf.html].

[18] Discussed by General Alfred M. Gray at the OSS's internet site: gopher://ossnet, in an article "Global intelligence challenges in the 90's."

[19] Figures cited in Rona B. Stillman, John B. Stephenson, Keith A. Rhodes, Kirk J. Daubenspeck, Patrick R. Dugan, and Christina T. Chaplain, "Information security: computer attacks at Department of Defense pose increasing risks," General Accounting Office, May 1996.

[20] Roger C. Molander, Andrew S. Riddle, Peter A. Wilson, "Infor-

mation warfare: a two edge sword," *Rand Research Review*, Fall 1995. Also on the Rand corporation Web site: www. rand.org/.

21 *Ibid.*, Chapter 0:3.1.

22 Clarence A. Robinson Jr., "High volume network shares information over vast reaches," *Signal Magazine*, October 1996.

23 DISA Web site: http://www.disa.mil/disahome.html.

24 Cited by Barbara Starr, "Deutch plans new direction for CIA," *Jane's Defense Weekly*, July 8, 1995.

25 Rona B. Stillman *et al.*, *op. cit.*, Chapter 2:2.1.

26 As quoted in Pat Cooper, "Organized crime hackers jeopardize security of U.S.," *Defense News*, October 3, 1994.

Chapter 8

1 Bruno Martinet and Yves-Michel Marti, *L'intelligence économique. Les yeux et les oreilles de l'entreprise*, Editions d'organisation, Paris, 1995, p. 236.

2 ATR is a European aerospace consortium comprising Aeritalia, Aérospatiale and British Aerospace, whose planes are referred to as ATRs.

3 Free Burma: www.irn.org/burma/total.html.
Soros Foundations: www.soros.org/burma/frntotal.html.
Total also deals with the subject on its own website: www.total.com/fr/cahier/yadana.html.

4 Internet site: http://verity.com/products.html.

5 *Parataxis:* The juxtaposition of clauses or phrases without the use of coordinating or subordinating conjunctions, as *It was cold; the snows came. Anaphora:* The deliberate repetition of a word or phrase at the beginning of several successive verses, clauses, or paragraphs; for example, "We shall fight on the beaches, we shall fight on the landing grounds, we shall fight in the fields and in the streets, we shall fight in the hills" (Winston S. Churchill). *Tropes:* The figurative use of a word or expression, as metaphor or hyperbole. *Diachronies:* Diachronic (i.e., historical) arrangement or analysis, especially of language. *Hapax legomenon:* A word or form that occurs only once in the recorded corpus of a given language.

6 Internet site: http://www.yahoo.com/.

7 Internet site: http://lycos.cs.cmu.edu/.

[8] Pierre Lévy and Michel Authier, with preface by Michel Serres, *Les arbies de connaissance*, La Découverte, Paris, 1992.

[9] Web site: http://www.mit.edu:8001/afs/athena.mit.edu/user/r/e/rei/wroot/people/mkgray/net/.

[10] Internet site: http://atlas.irit.fr/cgi-bin/visite.

[11] Touafiq Dkaki and Bernard Dousset, "Competitive intelligence: data extraction and analysis," *International Symposium on Intelligent Data Analysis* (IDA'95), Baden–Baden, August 17–19, 1995.

[12] Christian Harbulot, *La machine de guerre économique: États-Unis, Japon, Europe,* Économica, Paris, 1992, p. 91.

[13] Web site: http://ns.krollassociates.com/.

[14] Web site: http://www.fuld.com/body.html.

[15] Web site: http://www.ktyson.com/.

[16] Web site: http://www.indigo-net.com/. This site features an outstanding, well-protected payment interface.

[17] Coopers and Lybrand: http://www.colybrand.com/; Deloitte and Touche: http://www.dttus.com/; Arthur Andersen: http://www.arthurandersen.com/; Ernst and Young: http://www.ey.com; KPMG-Peat Marwick: web site: http://www.kpmg.com/; Price Waterhouse::http://www.pw.com/].

[18] *Intelligence Newsletter,* Number 302, January 2, 1997.

[19] Service canadien de sécurité et de renseignements.

[20] *Intelligence Newsletter,* Number 209, January 21, 1993.

[21] Advanced materials and coatings, advanced transportation and engine technology, aeronautics systems, aerospace, armaments and energetic materials, biotechnology, chemical and biological systems, computer software and hardware, defense and armaments technology, directed and kinetic energy systems, electronics, energy research, guidance, navigation and vehicle control, information systems, information warfare, manufacturing and fabrication, manufacturing processes, marine systems, materials, nuclear systems, semiconductors, sensors and lasers, signature control, space systems, telecommunications, weapons effects and countermeasures. (From the National Counterintelligence Center Annual report to Congress, May 1996).

[22] *Counterintelligence News and Development,* Number 1, November 1995. On the NACIC Web site: http://www.nacic.gov.

Chapter 9

[1] *Los Angeles Times*, July 25, 1994,

[2] Web site: http://www.transparency.de/links/.

[3] Ron Brown, a close friend of President Clinton, died in April 1996 in the crash of a U.S. Air Force plane while leading a delegation of American businessmen to Croatia.

[4] Claude Silberzahn, *Au cœur du secret, 1500 jours aux commandes de la DGSE 1989/1993*, Fayard, Paris, 1995, p. 171.

[5] In July 1985, a French special forces unit acting under the aegis of the DGSE sunk the flagship of the Greenpeace fleet, the *Rainbow Warrior*, in port in Auckland, New Zealand. The ship was preparing to sail for a nuclear site in Mururoa. A Greenpeace photographer was found dead in the wreckage. The French government initially denied any involvement in the incident. Defense Minister Charles Hernu eventually stepped down. The head of the secret services, admiral Pierre Lacoste, was dismissed.

[6] Pierre Lacoste, "Les entreprises doivent apprendre à se protéger," *Capital*, February 1995.

[7] *Time Magazine*, May 28, 1990.

[8] *Los Angeles Times*, February 3, 1993.

[9] *Los Angeles Times*, July 15, 1995.

[10] Robert Keatley, "Staying competitive has new meaning, thanks to the CIA. Spy agency offers services to corporate America: no more 'Mr. Nice Guy,'" *Wall Street Journal*, January 18, 1994.

[11] *Los Angeles Times*, July 15, 1995.

[12] *Ibid.*

[13] *Ibid.*

[14] *Ibid.*

[15] Robert Dreyfuss, "The CIA has opened a global Pandora's box by spying on foreign competitors of American companies," *Mother Jones*, 1994.

[16] The French and the Americans had been supporting different sides of this struggle, the United States helping the Tutsis and France helping the Hutus, during the time leading up to the massacre of the Tutsis by the Hutus.

[17] While in France, American agents did what all foreign agents do in foreign lands: they tried to recruit agents from the other side, as high up as the office of the prime minister. These maneuvers were less about the theft of information

than the supposed comfort that comes from having a fly on the wall.

[18] Then a diplomat, Bernard Guillet was caught by the CIA, *in flagrante delicto*, recuperating sensitive documents.

[19] James Risen, "Clinton reportedly orders CIA to focus on trade espionage intelligence," *Los Angeles Times*, July 23, 1995.

[20] Philippe Baumard, "From noticing to making sense. Using intelligence to develop strategy," *International Journal of Intelligence and Counter-intelligence*, Volume 7, Number 1, Spring 1994.

[21] Internet site: http://www.scip.org.

[22] Pierre Lacoste, "Les entreprises doivent apprendre à se protéger," *op. cit.*

[23] Robert Steele, "Talking point to point to the director of central intelligence," Proceedings of the Second Symposium on National Security and National Competitiveness: Open Sources Solutions, Washington, DC, 1993.

[24] Robert Steele, "Reinventing intelligence: holy grail or mission impossible?" *International Journal of Intelligence and Counter-Intelligence*, Volume 7, Number 1, March 1994.

[25] In France, the penal code prohibits the collection of "open information" for the benefit of a foreign power—strange but true.

[26] Elf Atochem is the chemical wing of the petroleum giant Elf Aquitaine. It did $11 billion in sales in 1995 and employs thirty-three thousand people.

[27] François Jakobiak, *Pratique de la veille technologique*, Éditions d'organisation, Paris, 1991, p. 28.

[28] Christian Harbulot, *La machine de guerre économique: États-Unis, Japon, Europe, op. cit.*, p. 88.

[29] Bob Johnstone, "Turf wars," *Wired*, June 1994.

[30] Nicholas Negroponte, *Being Digital*, Alfred A. Knopf, New York, 1995. We used the January 1996 paperback edition, First Vintage Books, p. 198.

[31] Kent E. Calder, "Japan in danger of being bypassed in the information age," *Asia Times*, November 18, 1996. *Asia Times* Web site: http://www.asiatimes.com/.

[32] Takano Hajime, "Only the spirit of independence can sustain the Internet," March 6, 1996, on the Web site of Tokyo Kaleidoscoop: http://www.smn.co.jp:80/TEXT/index.html.

[33] *Les Echos*, January 10, 1997.

[34] Economic survey of Japan, monthly economic report, guide

to Office of trade and investment, economic research institute, consumer protection policy. Web site: http://epa.go.jp/.

[35] Eishi Katsura, "Citoyens nippons sous surveillance," *Le Monde diplomatique,* February 1995.

[36] Internet site: http://www.twics.com/~COMLINE/database. html.

[37] Christian Harbulot, "Intelligence économique japonaise: de la sous-information à la sur-information," *La Lettre d'Asie,* Number 24, July 31, 1995.

[38] Keisuke Okumuzi, "An overview of the Japanese databases," at Internet site http//:www.dpc.or.jp/.

Chapter 10

[1] Electronic address: president@white-house.gov. The White House has its own Web site, the most interesting element of which is undoubtedly the "meow" of the white house cat. Internet site: http://www.whitehouse.gov.

[2] Pierre Lévy, *Collective Intelligence,* Plenum Trade, New York, 1997.

[3] *Ibid.*

[4] Pierre Briançon, "Quotidiens branches," *Libération,* April 28, 1995.

[5] Web site: http://wsj.com/ For fifty dollars a year you can subscribe to a customized, interactive version of the newspaper.

[6] Internet site: www.nytimes.com. Subscriptions to the electronic edition are fairly expensive (thirty-five dollars per month), and access to the site is impossible without a subscription.

[7] Web site: http://washingtonpost.com/.

[8] Web site: http://www.latimes.com/.

[9] Internet site: http://www.netfrance.com/Libe/.

[10] Web site: http://www.lwmonde.fr/.

[11] Web site: http://www.webdo.ch/webactu/webactu_presse. html.

[12] Pointcast: http://www.pointcast.com/ MSNBC: http:// wwwmsnbc.com/news/default.asp.

[13] Cited by Suneel Ratan, "A new divide between haves and have-nots?" *Time,* special issue on the Internet, April 1995.

[14] Barbara Kantrowitz, "The information gap," *Newsweek*, March 21, 1994.

[15] Mahdi Elmandjra, "L'impact de l'environnement socioculturel sur le développement des technologies de l'information," *Terminal*, Number 62, Winter 1993.

[16] Michel Raffoul, "Bengalore, silicon valley à l'indienne," *Le Monde diplomatique*, January 1997. Web site: www.ina.fr/CP/MondeDiplo/

[17] Paul Virilio, "Nous allons vers des Tchernobyl informatiques," *Terminal*, Number 62, Winter 1993. Virilio, a specialist in the analysus of "speed" in all its manifestations, has further specialized in a little niche that might be termed "Netphobia": "I think that the infosphere—the sphere of information—is going to impose itself on the geosphere. We are going to be living in a reduced world. The capacity of interactivity is going to reduce the world to nearly nothing. In fact, there is already a speed pollution, which reduces the world to nothing. In the near future, people will feel enclosed in a small environment. They will have a feeling of confinement in the world, which will certainly be at the limit of tolerability, by virtue of the speed of information. If I were to offer you a last thought—interactivity is to real space what radioactivity is to the atmosphere." From the article "Speed pollution," *Wired*, May 1996.

[18] Internet site: http://www.econet.apc.org/econet/.

[19] Internet site: http://www.igc.apc.org/conflictnet/.

[20] Internet site: http://www.glasnet.ru/brochure.html.

[21] Carlos-Alberto Afonso, "Réseaux électroniques et action politique. Au service de la société civile," *Le Monde diplomatique*, July 1994.

[22] Mercy Wambui, "Internauts on the rise," *Econews Africa*, Volume 4, Number 13. Web site: http://www.web.apc.org/~econews/.

Epilogue

[1] The vice president's Internet site: vice-president@whitehouse.gov.

[2] Pierre Lévy, *Collective Intelligence*, Plenum Trade, New York, p. XX.

[3] Nicholas Negroponte, *Being Digital*, Alfred A. Knopf, New York, 1995, p. 181.

Acknowledgments

This book, the result of a long investigation, was published first in France in 1995. I would like to thank my editor, the ever rigorous and attentive Francois Gèze, who was my first reader. In the translation of this work, we set in motion all the resources of the Internet, making many round trips between Paris and the U.S. I want to express my gratitude to my translator Gui Massai; Erika Goldman, of Plenum Publishing, knew how to tap into the resources of her indulgent francophilia to smooth out, efficiently and with humor, the difficulties of the enterprise. I know how much this publication owes to her, and can't thank her enough. Several expert readers—Dr. Dorothy E. Denning, Jean-Louis Gassée, Chris Goggans, Dr. Robbin Laird, Winn Schwartau, and Robert D. Steele among them—have gone over the manuscript in part or entirely and made remarks and suggestions. They were very helpful, and I'm extremely grateful to them. If any errors have remained in the text, I take full responsibility for them.

Index